Life's Little Lessons

GOOD, bad,
or InDiFfErEnT

That Get You from Here to There

- BY SHEILA R. KING -

W
WELSTAR PUBLICATIONS
• BROOKLYN, NEW YORK •

Published by Welstar Publications, LLC.
Horace Batson, Ph.D., Publisher
628 Lexington Avenue, Brooklyn, NY 11221.
Phone: (646) 409-0340
Fax: (313) 453-6554
E-mail: drbatson@optonline.net
ISBN: 978-0-938503-29-3

Managing Editor, Horace Batson, Ph.D.
Book Design/Typography, Sheila R. Knight
Text set in Calibri

Life's Little Lessons

GOOD, bad,
or InDiFfErEnT

That Get You from Here to There

—⁓—

- BY SHEILA R. KING -

Table of Contents

"And at midnight there was a cry made, Behold, the bridegroom cometh;
go ye out to meet him. Then all those virgins arose,
and trimmed their lamps."

MATTHEW 25:6-7 (KJV)

Foreword

~ By Jeanette Espinoza ~

Author of Both Sides of the Fence, and The Weighting Game

———————————— —ɯ— ————————————

From the moment I met Sheila King Knight, I knew I was in the presence of someone who possessed the ability to change the world. The words dynamic, innovative, and creative immediately come to mind when I think of this incredible woman. Spiritually grounded with an ability to impart knowledge in an effective, humorous, and thought-provoking way, Sheila quickly became the unofficial adviser at work during our course of employment with an insurance company. Her cubicle became a safe haven for our co-workers and myself to share secrets and experiences in our personal lives and to have the opportunity to obtain knowledge from Sheila, from both a realistic and spiritual perspective. The gentle but truthful advice that she gave so unselfishly, served to enrich our lives and broaden our scope of understanding for life's everyday trials.

As Sheila and I began to get to know one another better, we learned that we shared something in common: our love for the written word. I discussed the details of the book I had written with her and inquired if she had ever thought to pen some of her heartfelt, no-nonsense thoughts on love, relationships, and the common situations we all face, that she so regularly counseled myself and others on, in an effort to help us gain a greater understanding of life's lessons. When she divulged the fact that she had always had a desire to write, I immediately knew that we were having a discussion of something that would soon far surpass anything that I could imagine and that the words of wisdom that I had coveted after knowing Sheila for years, would finally be available for all to benefit from.

Life's Little Lessons-GOOD, bad, or InDiFfErEnT That Get You from Here to There is not just a book, but a journey. Sheila skillfully and shamelessly shares situations that we all encounter as we go about the business of living and loving and gives not only her own insightful perspective on the situation presented, but she masterfully ties in the word of God to each instance. That's right, I'm not sure you heard that so I'll say it one more time: She ties in the word of God to each situation so that you not only get a realistic and fresh outlook on the situation, but you also receive confirmation from the Master of all situations, to aid in further understanding of how to best cope with the issue being discussed. After months of research and polling various people from different walks of life, Sheila was able to compile a book filled with life lessons dealing with topics such as interpersonal relationships, infidelity, conflicts between family and friends, the trials and tribulations of dating and trying to find "the one," the complex issues faced by married couples regarding finances, trust, and continued compatibility, and many, many more instances that help us to look deep into our own hearts and souls and come face to face with the challenges we encounter on a daily basis. *Life's Little Lessons - GOOD, bad, or InDiFfErEnT That Get You from Here to There* is a smartly-written guide to assisting the reader with daring to delve deeper into his self-conscious in order to get to the root of any problem. This book also provides the necessary tools to aid in finding the remedy in any situation to allow us to get to the ultimate space of peace and contentment in our lives.

Sheila has often said that she does not consider herself a conduit of greatness and rather always gives the glory and praise to God for her talents and accomplishments. It is clear after reading the content of this book that God most certainly had a plan in mind for Sheila. It is evident that He led her throughout her life and allowed her to gain just the right combination of knowledge and skill to be able to use her as a vessel to impart those invaluable lessons to others. Just knowing such an amazing and powerful woman and having the ultimate privilege of being in the front row to hear the indispensable knowledge and insight from her on a daily basis, has indeed changed my life. She has helped me to maintain an open mind concerning my own life's issues and has given me the ability to view situations from the perspective of everyone involved-and not just my own. It will be extremely beneficial to the world when the knowledge that I've been so blessed to have at my discretion becomes available to all who truly need it. Sheila's work has just begun and I will venture to predict that this will be one of many of her works that will serve to heal, strengthen, and change the world, one situation at a time.

Introduction

~ By Sheila King Knight ~
Life Relationship Coach

———————————— —m— ————————————

"Oh, I say and I say it again, Ya been had! Ya been took! Ya been hoodwinked! Bamboozled! Led astray! Run amok! This is what He does..." The situations compiled in this Christian self-help book about the realities of everyday life are legitimate; the names have been concealed to protect the individuals, as all aren't as transparent as some in discussing their mistakes as it relates to marriage, divorce, dating, singleness, parenting, test, trials or tribulations, or just things that affect our daily lives. I come as naked and unashamed as I can before you and God, and have openly shared my imperfections with as many as will listen, and now read.

We hope that by living and sharing the realities of these situations that it will help you to avoid making some of the same mistakes we did. This book will be a real-life tool to help you get to where you need to be without coming to those dead end roadblocks every time. I've always heard that experience was the best teacher, but if I had something like this guide to help me a bit along the way, it would have made some of my struggles a little easier, and less disappointing. I wouldn't trade the test, trials or tribulations of where I've been for one minute because they have all come to make me a stronger and better person today. I have found that now that I'm a fully grown woman (can't believe I'm actually saying that) I see things differently than I did when I was in my twenties or thirties-it's called experience and wisdom, all wrapped up in one package. I take responsibility for all of my actions now. At one time or another in life many people have uttered the phrase, "I wanna be just like you when I grow up." My advice to these people is to be who God has created them to be and to not try to be like someone else. I can honestly say that I didn't want to be just like me, because I didn't like what I had done and some of the places I had gone, but I can say through God's grace that I'm thankful for the person I've become today. Nuff Sed!

The best thing that was birthed through all of my stuff was my testimonies, and I thank God daily for them, as I'm now able to share them with you. You do know that we are blessed to be a blessing to someone else through our testimonies: "And they overcame him by the blood of the Lamb, and by the word of their testimony; and they loved not their lives unto the death," (Rev 12:11). I had to learn that my testimony wasn't for me-it was for someone else. God had to drop that into my spiritual in-box. My prayer is that you will use these situations to help you move from Here to There, recognizing that God is always present and He will be with you through any and all you will ever go through in life. Trust and depend on Him, because He will never let you down. You may fall, but I encourage you to get back up, and brush yourself off as He carries you through the storms of life. Never stop seeking, asking or knocking- "Ask, and it shall be given you; seek, and ye shall find; knock, and it shall be opened unto you: For every one that asketh receiveth; and he that seeketh findeth; and to him that knocketh it shall be opened," (Matt 7:7-8).

There are so many lessons to learn, like: "The battle is not yours, it's the Lord's," "To whom much is given, much is required," "Only what you do for Christ will last," "I'm so glad trouble don't last always," and so many more. Hold them dear to your heart and when troubles come-and they will surely come-you'll already be equipped with your amour and prepared to handle them with or without someone there to hold your hand. The one thing that I truly appreciate about God is that He knows what you need and will ensure you have it during that time of trouble. Be it a friend or significant other, He will provide just what you need to make it through troubled waters, because He is that bridge over troubled waters. Be encouraged and expect the great things God has to offer you, knowing that "The glory of this latter house shall be greater than of the former, saith the LORD of hosts: and in this place will I give peace, saith the LORD of hosts," (Hag 2:9). I would also like to take this opportunity to introduce you to Him. If you don't already know Him, let me tell you, He's a way-maker, a way out of no way, a comforter and a provider, too. He'll be to you what no other person can or ever will be. How does one receive salvation? The Bible says, "For by grace are ye saved through faith; and that not of yourselves: it is the gift of God: Not of works, lest any man should boast," (Eph 2:8-9). You can receive the gift of salvation, through this simple sinner's prayer: "Lord, I believe you died on the cross for my sins. I am a sinner, I have sinned against you, and I ask you for your forgiveness. Lord, I place my trust in you as my Lord and my Savior, please come into my life." You must confess that He is Lord and invite Him in; then you are saved. Invite Him in today. It's the most important invitation you'll ever extend and the best gift you'll ever receive.

Writing this book has truly changed my life. It's taught me to be more honest with myself, making it easier to be more transparent with those around me. It's taught me to forgive, forget and to release. I've learned that as men and women, we really do have some of the same struggles in life. I've also learned that I'm no better than the next person, regardless of my race, sex, religion, national origin, disability, age, etc...all that employment discrimination mumbo-jumbo stuff that I've learned in my 22 years plus experience as a Human Resources Professional. I laugh, cry and bleed just like everyone else. If God is no respecter of persons (Acts 10:34), then why should I be? It's His saving grace that makes the difference. He says in His word, "Judge not that ye be not judged," (Matt 7:1-5). Why are you looking at the mote in my eye when you have a whole beam in your own? I mean, I have skeletons, but you have bodies in your closet. Lol! People are so hypocritical and it all needs to stop, but it can't stop if they don't have a clue as to who they really are, or whom they really belong to. It reminds me of Marvin Sapp's song, "The Best in Me," in which he describes his relationship with God saying, "…See He's mine, and I am His, it doesn't matter what I did, He only sees me for who I am." I'm so glad that I've taken the time to at least try and get it right. I'm not all that, nor have I arrived. I'm still growing daily, but I'm further along than I once was, and surely am not what I used to be. All praise be to God! Before you know where you're going, you have to understand where you've been.

The book begins with Negative and Positive Remarks that Affect Our Progress and Key Parts of Your Character that Make up Who You Are. What people say to or about you has a significant impact on your growth. Next, there are those Thoughts, Quotes, Scriptures and Comments that Motivate Your Growth. The guts of this book are of course, the Real Life Situations that Get You from Here to There. I've provided illustrations that detail actual situations, my initial thoughts behind them and a scripture reference that drives the moral of the story home. Doing things God's way is the one and only way to live life more abundantly. I have also provided space for you to analyze and write down how you would have handled the situation. One thing is for sure: you never know how you're really going to handle a situation until you are faced with it. It's never good to say, "I wouldn't do that" or "I would have handled it this way," when in reality you really don't know how you'll handle a situation until you've lived it.

The final phase of the book is called the Relationship Tool Box: In Preparation for Marriage, which deals with the overview of a relationship; Whatcha' Lookin 4, Honesty Test: Would You Marry Yourself?, From a Man's Point of View, The Keys to a Lasting Courtship and Marriage, and What it Takes for a Long-lasting Relationship are just a few of the topics we will explore. What I've discovered in writing this book and reading through all of the scenarios, is that people don't want to work at relationships anymore-they just really want someone to tell them what to do. If that's the case, you'll never learn from your mistakes. Secondly, as my Pastor said during a sermon about marriage: "Most marriages aren't working because we've stopped doing it God's way."

Another thing that I've realized is that we need to get back to the nuts and bolts of how life should be lived and ask those basic but necessary questions while we're dating to get the results we want or need for the next phase (marriage). It's called interviewing people, and you can't ever do enough of it before jumping the broom. It is unrealistic and pure insanity to meet a person today and marry them tomorrow, without getting to know them thoroughly. When we finally do get married, we need to make an attempt to work out some of our discrepancies before heading to divorce court, and filing for irreconcilable differences-what's that about any way?

The top reasons that marriages fail or end in divorce are due to issues concerning: finances, commitment, infidelity, communication and the family. Here's what Lawyers.com had to say about irreconcilable differences : "In most states, a spouse may get a no-fault divorce based on a breakdown of the marriage. Some states refer to this breakdown of a marriage as "irreconcilable differences." It means you and your spouse can't agree on basic, fundamental issues involving the marriage or your family, and you never will agree… When a divorce is based on irreconcilable differences, any wrongdoing by the one spouse or the other doesn't matter. It's simply a statement by both spouses that the marriage won't work any longer. You don't need to prove that your spouse was to blame for the failure of your marriage to get a no-fault divorce based on irreconcilable differences. A court may grant you a divorce if it finds that you and your spouse can no longer live together due to your irreconcilable differences." My brain is on overload-too much information. If you had done what you were supposed to do in the first place, then you wouldn't have to go through all of that stuff now. Don't let life's situations become a pill that's too hard to swallow. Oy vey, awful stuff!

The last part of the book gives you an opportunity to record your progress by using the journal provided. If you don't already journal, it's a good idea to start because it helps to get your thoughts out of your head and onto paper. Your thoughts become more realistic when you can see them in a written format. Life is a journey, so much transpires, but you can write it down. Don't forget to review your journal from time to time to see how you've grown. Growth is a process and you'll be amazed at how much you grow through the tests, trials and tribulations of life. My hope is that the information contained in this book will help you to truly get from Here to There, recognizing that the "T" that makes "here," there, are those tests, trials and tribulations that you must go through in order to be able to stand once you arrive at your intended destination.

May you use the Little Lessons learned from these situations and relationship tools to assist you in successful living, whether it be in singleness, dating someone who makes your heart smile or in marriage. Even if your desire is to never marry, it's about being happy in whatever state you choose to live in. Paul says it best: "Not that I speak in respect of want: for I have learned, in whatsoever state I am, therein to be content," (Phil 4:11). Do all things decently and in order (1 Co 14:40) as directed by God, using the morals, values and principles He has instilled in you.

It's about forgiving and healing those hurts so you can live an abundant life (John 10:10). It's about enjoying life from the inside out, and not the outside in. The way you live will always be evident in your walk and in the way you talk. You know how you can tell someone that you're doing ok, but that's not what they see on your face? "It's written all over your face, you don't have to say a word." Free your mind and your heart will follow. Stop carrying around all that "stuff" like a bag lady with no place to go. Stop weighing yourself down with all that unnecessary baggage. Let it go, for real! Set realistic and achievable goals for yourself. Implement a plan for your life. Remember, you either plan to succeed or you plan to fail-let the latter not be the one you choose. Failure is not an option.

Decide to get around people who are smarter than you are who can teach you a "new thing" (I thank you Pastor Curney, for those words). Stop living that old life that's gotten you nowhere at all. You are better, you are smarter, and your life is brighter. Walk into your destiny, live the abundant life, take authority and claim your rightful inheritance.

Our Father is rich in houses and in land. Baby, go get what's yours.
Live, laugh, love and enjoy doing it. It's called freedom-and it does live
at my address.

Acknowledgement

TO GOD BE THE GLORY
FOR THE THINGS HE HAS DONE

———————————— ～Ⅲ～ ————————————

Life is always about moving forward. No matter what's happening, you still have to learn to pick yourself up, dust yourself off, and move on. It really is about getting from Here to There, and unless you've been here, you're never going to survive being there. I'll say it again, the "T" that makes "here," there are those tests, trials, and tribulations that you must go through. A good friend shared that with me while I was going through my own test...thanks Chester D. T. Baldwin, much love, as that discussion changed my life. In life, you never stop learning. Each test is a testimony waiting to be birthed or shared with someone else who will have a similar experience (not in the same manner). I learned the order of the process: "first the test, then the testimony-you can't have one without the other." It's also important to understand that a test is never a mistake, but it's God's way of getting our attention for His glory. Whatever place God brings you to, He makes provision for you there.

My testimony began in September 1995, as this was the biggest spiritual test of my life. See, that's when God shared with me that it wasn't about me, or anything that I could do. At that point, He began to break and make me into the person that I have become today. When I surrendered my all to Him, He began to take complete control of my life. During that process of reconstruction, I still had a lot of growing to do. As I think back, it wasn't a pleasant place to be in. The enemy was trying to rob me of where God was trying to take me. That old enemy is so cunning; he always tries to keep you in an accused state, but he's not smarter than the Creator, who knows you and your destiny. Jeremiah 1:5 declares, "Before I formed thee in the belly I knew thee; and before thou camest forth out of the womb I sanctified thee, and I ordained thee a prophet unto the nations." That's what God said-get thee behind me Satan (Mt 16:23).

I had to live through loss of a job, financial struggles, marriage, divorce, heartache, and many other disappointments, but I made it through by the grace of Almighty God, leaning on many scriptures, including Philippians 4:6-8. For at that point, He taught me not to be anxious, "...but in everything by prayer and supplication with thanksgiving let your requests be made known unto God," (v.6). He helped me to focus on things that were just, pure, lovely, and good (v.8), while He moved me according to His plan and purpose for my life. It wasn't easy, but "...thanks be unto God, which always causeth us to triumph in Christ, and maketh manifest the savour of his knowledge by us in every place," (2 Cor 2:14). I'm still here to tell the story! You can do all things through Christ who gives you strength (Phil 4:13); all being just a three-letter word, but it encompasses everything that you could ever think or imagine and more.

Prior to 1995, I was in a very unhealthy and unsafe relationship with a man that I loved with all of my heart and soul. I loved this man more than life itself. That relationship ended up causing me much heartache and pain. I was ultimately subjected to emotional and physical abuse, but I loved this man to the point that God Himself, had to come and rescue me from that situation. For many years, I found myself robbed of all that God wanted for my life.

Now, let's fast forward to February 14, 1997, when I married my "knight in shining armor"-the man that I loved and respected, but wasn't in love with (there is a difference). To that man I say "Godspeed," and I pray that he finds forgiveness in his heart and is able to move on and find true love for himself one day, as I have. I now realize that was one of the main reasons for a lot of the problems in my marriage. And to all those that I've had the opportunity to like, date or even love, I hope I didn't leave a bitter taste in your heart, but instead, a spirit of God's love that you are now able to share with someone else.

Every man isn't for every woman and every woman isn't for every man. If you don't get that now, you might catch it on the way home tomorrow-it took me a minute to get it, too. When I finally realized that, I was able to move on with an even greater understanding of this relationship "thing." I understand it enough now to know what I want and need, and I'm not settling for anything less, any longer. Now, all of those missed or lost relationships make me think about the title of Beyoncé's song, "Best Thing I Never Had." As I reflect, I realize that bad relationship turned out to be the best thing I never had. I am so over it, and have moved on to a better and fulfilling place in my life. I'm a living testament that God "…will restore to you the years that the locust hath eaten," (Joel 2:25).

I'm grateful today to be able to look at the woman in the mirror and be honest with myself. I made a lot of mistakes that I didn't know how to correct because of where I had been mentally and emotionally in my previous relationships. I wasn't able to move forward; I was stuck. Nobody ever teaches you how to be married, or how to date correctly, for that matter. See, if you never deal with the root cause of your issues, you'll never be able to move forward to a sound solution. Looking back, I recognize that I grew up most from that 17-year relationship with my ex-husband. I learned how to be truest to me. With a clear heart and mind I can say, "Thank you God, for helping me to see that the glass was neither half-full nor half-empty. Thank you God, for removing the gray areas in my life and allowing me to live in black, white and Technicolor. Thank you God, for helping me to remove those rose-colored glasses that I had worn for so long. Most importantly, thank you God, for helping me to forgive so that I could be released to live a wonderfully joyous and complete life of faith, hope and love. Like radio host and comedian, Steve Harvey says, "Straight, with no chaser." Today, my glass is full; full of the joy that only comes from God up above. To Him, I give all glory and honor, and I am forever grateful for that unmerited favor and peace that passes all understanding. I'm most blessed to present to you my gift from all the things God had to take me through to finally get me to this place; a safer place, a place of peace, and a place of rest. Now, I present to you *Life's Little Lessons-GOOD, bad, or InDiFfErEnT That Get You from Here to There.*

"Life's Little Lessons - GOOD, bad, or InDiFfErEnT
That Get You from Here to There"

"If you think that I'm not what I'm supposed to be,

oh, please be a little patient with me and if you wait a little while

and give me a chance I bet, you don't have to worry nor fret, I'm

going to be alright because God's not through with me yet."

FROM THE PEN OF

Brenda Waters

~ R.I.P. ~

Dedications

~ With Love To ~

———————————— —◊◊◊— ————————————

Nadine King, Eddie "Cleanhead" Vinson, Jessie Mae & John Walker, Nerlon "Jimmy" Benson, Pearl Renee Bennett, Kenneth LaRue Brown, Lillian "Penny" Akins and many others who loved, paved the way and prayed for me.

First and foremost, God you are so awesome. Thank you for the gift of salvation and the understanding of why it isn't about us or anything that we can do-it's truly about you.   Thanks to all who helped me make this book a reality, by opening up and sharing those painful tests, trials and tribulations in your life to help someone else come out of the dark and into the marvelous light. I am humbled by you sharing your testimonies with me. To my sisters, Carol, Ramona, Rosalind and Wanda, and the Process-affectionately known as "Women under Construction" (the WUC's), if I had never been in that place, I wouldn't be here today, as that's where it all started, as well as the introduction to "The

Challenge or the Gift of Being Single." What a wonderful journey that was. We were able to introduce to Mt. Sinai Missionary Baptist Church (Austin, TX) a unique alternative to a traditional Sunday School Class that taught us about life and relationships. Thank you Pastor A.W. Anthony Mays for your willingness to let us do it and for letting us know that we didn't have "that gift." I now fully understand what "Thanks be unto God for his unspeakable gift," (2 Cor 9:15) really means. Thank you for your teaching, for it helped me in ways that I can never explain and helped me to get past so many road blocks. I'll never forget how you and "The Mount" were there for me during the loss of my mother. You did exactly what a church family is supposed to do; you provided comfort, love and support to me and my family, and for that, we are forever grateful. Much love to you, Sister Mays and the entire Mays family.

To Pastor Gaylon Clark, Lead Pastor of Greater Mt Zion (Austin, TX), you are an awesome, true man of God. Thank you for how you helped me to finally make that much needed move in my life and to free myself from some over 20 years of "stuff" that was quickly leading me to spiritual death. Thank you for "Dating Backwards, Finding Your Boo." What an awesome interpretation of the issues we go through as single and married people, which we never address, but continue living through like everything is ok. That's a bestseller waiting to be sold. Thank you for giving me that wonderful book, If You Want to Walk on Water, You've Got to Get Out of the Boat, by John Ortberg, which helped me with my "Peter" experiences. I recognized that everybody has them and that fear really does stop one from moving forward. Much love to you and Kathy.

True friend-how many of us really have them? To my "joined-at-the-hip" sisters, Carmen Lacount and Linda Williams, words can never express what you have been to me. I think I'll call us, "Sisters in the Name of Love." You and your entire family have shown unconditional love to me since we first met, back at Albert Sidney Johnston High School in the seventies (now that's really back in the day). I can truly say that we are friends to the end. We don't talk daily but whenever I call, you are right there. To Charlene, my road doggy...Girrrrl, we've been through thick and thin, and are still going, like that "Ever Ready Battery Bunny." Im'ma need for you to go by Linda's and bring a bin when you come to the ATL again. ROTFLOL!

To Michael and Shaune Littleton, thank you, thank you, thank you for caring about my wellbeing. It's nice to know that there are still some good people out there who just care and that would be you guys. Shaune, you know it ain't reality until I tell you, and you never judge me. To Denice with a "c", gurlie you can make me laugh like nobody else, and you be serious about what you be telling me too, and I be laughing my butt off. I'll never forget, "moo, moo," and you know what I'm talking about. To my partner in the Ministry, Chief Servant Vera Young, aka "Kingdom Girl," thanks for the many opportunities to minister through song when you minister in the Word. You are off the chain, "Kingdom Girl." Praise is your most elite garment, "Cuz ain't no party like the Holy Ghost party, cuz the Holy Ghost party don't stop." I'm looking forward to seeing where God's going to take The Renaissance Church and Saturday Night Live. I'm humbled by the opportunity to be a key part of your vision.

To my ATL Connection, thank you Andrea, Carla, Clifton, Coretta, Dana, DJ, Donna, Erica, James, Jim-T, Kelly, LaShun, LeVoice, Lydia, Margo, Mary, Pat, Sam, Stephanie, Tanji, Tasha, Tonja and many others too numerous to name, for being that inspiration in my life for such a time as this. I love you guys with my whole heart.

To my Pastor and wife Jimmy and Dr. LaShun Robinson, I'm so excited about where Purpose World Church is going, and grateful to be a part of the vision. Miracles, Signs and Wonders.

To Pastor, Jesse Curney III, New Mercies Christian Church (Lilburn, GA) for preaching the true and living word. Thanks for not being afraid to say, "Exit! Exit! Exit!" when one doesn't want to hear or accept the truth and nothing but the truth. Thank you for also being transparent about your life experiences, as a lot of my inspiration to write came from your messages. "Preach, I believe you do, and do it well." I love it when you say, "If they said it, it's 99.99 percent true." I can appreciate the honesty. It is the truth that we know that sets us free! To First Lady, Aleana Curney, I appreciate your spirit and love for God-it does not go unnoticed, what a crowned jewel you really are. It was a great nine years under your leadership.

To the wind beneath my wings, my hero, and brother, William "Bill" King, for loving me unconditionally to the point that it really doesn't matter, because you just gone love me anyway. We share so many special moments, and boyyy you can play those keys and write like nobody I've ever known. The world still needs to hear the "Bride Song-When You Come." How bout we do the CD Project next? You've made me feel special all of my life. I love you so much. Who wouldn't want to have a brother like you? You're the best!

To my other brother, Robert Terrell thanks for the relationship and special bond that we share. I have seen you grow the most through adversity. Stand stronger, and stand stronger. Keep on standing my brotha, keep on standing! You know I always say, "You don't have to stand tall, but you do have to stand up." I'm going to try and get married again, one day, so do you think we can live apart long enough for that to happen? I'm giving you side-eye on that one ;). Sweeeet!-insider! Only those close to us will understand…aww understand! I love you much, "baby bruh!"

To my baby, O'Kycha Green, thanks for giving me the opportunity of motherhood and for loving me in the same manner. It was all I thought it would be. I hope you have the opportunity to experience motherhood one day. To the one I lost, I'll never know what it would have been like, but I appreciate the God we serve for not allowing you to come into this world under the circumstances at that time. For, I would have been forever tied to a man that would have continued to keep me in bondage. God always knows best. He'll never give us more than we can bear.

To Elliott Murray I'm speechless at how you just took a conversation and turned it into a reality for me. I can't even begin to express my appreciation for you helping me to make one of my most promising dreams come true. We have a friendship that will never end.

Finally to the woman who prayed for me more than 15 minutes during our very first conversation and confirmed over 10 things in my spirit and we had never spoken before. My, My, My God has a way of bringing individuals into your life for a season, a reason and a lifetime. Thanks to you Vivian Bell, my dream of becoming an author is now a reality. May God also grant you the desires of your heart through the dreams of others. You are that dream builder that keeps on giving. It is my prayer that God would make you and Diamond Pieces Entertainment a household name for years to come.

Chapter One

Negative and Positive Remarks
That Affect Our Progress

"Life's Little Lessons - GOOD, bad, or InDiFfErEnT
That Get You from Here to There"

What have people said about you

that stopped or could have stopped your progress?

❦

*"Let the words of my mouth,
and the meditation of my heart, be acceptable in thy sight,
O LORD, my strength, and my redeemer."*

~ PSALMS 19:14 ~

"Life's Little Lessons - GOOD, bad, or InDiFfErEnT
That Get You from Here to There"

NEGATIVE AND POSITIVE REMARKS THAT AFFECT OUR PROGRESS

NEGATIVE EXPRESSIONS	POSITIVE EXPRESSIONS
No one will ever want you	Oh, you're so pretty
You're too fat	You guys make a great couple
You're too black	You compliment one another well
You'll never make it	You have a great personality
You don't sing like…	Thanks for thinking of me
He/She's not the one for you	You have a good heart
I'm not with him/her, because if I was I would have to be out of my mind	There are so many things that I love about you
You'll never be anything	You make me feel brand new
If you come up against me, you'll lose	You light up my life
You're not my type	You make my heart skip a beat
I prefer a lighter/darker, man/woman	Where would I be without you in my life?
I don't chase women & I don't chase men so I guess we won't be chasing one another	I would die for you
Your physical features are too big/small	You make my life worth living
You're not good enough for him/her	You're doing it like that, wow!
You're too ugly	You have a million dollar smile
You're not pretty enough	I trust you with my life
You're not educated enough	You make me feel secure and wanted
You're not thin enough	I like your swag
I'm not in love with or seeking a relationship with you-it's just a sex thing	This world is better with you in it
I don't think this relationship will ever work	You're an awesome friend

"If you believe in me, then encourage and support me,

don't tear me down. "

Chapter Two

Key Parts of Your Character
That Make Up Who You Are

"Who are you and where did you come from?"

This is who I am

this is what I do.

KEY PARTS OF YOUR CHARACTER

That Make Up Who You Are

CHARACTER: The aggregate of features and traits that form the individual nature of some person or thing. One such feature or trait; characteristic. Moral or ethical quality.

BELIEF: Something believed; an opinion or conviction. Confidence in the truth or existence of something not immediately susceptible to rigorous proof.

CONFIDENCE: Full trust; belief in the powers, trustworthiness, or reliability of a person or thing. Belief in oneself and one's powers or abilities; self-confidence; self-reliance; assurance.

INTEGRITY: Adherence to moral and ethical principles; soundness of moral character; honesty.

MORALS: Pertaining to, or concerned with the principles or rules of right conduct or the distinction between right and wrong; ethical.

PERSONALITY: The visible aspect of one's character as it impresses others.   A person as an embodiment of a collection of qualities.

PRINCIPLE: An accepted or professed rule of action or conduct.

SELF-ESTEEM: A realistic respect for or favorable impression of oneself; self-respect.

VALUES: Relative worth, merit, or importance; to consider with respect to worth, excellence, usefulness, or importance; to regard or esteem highly.

Chapter One

Thoughts, Quotes, Scriptures and Comments

That Encourage and Motivate Your Growth

—⟪⟫—

· 9 ·

Here are just a few of the thoughts, quotes, scriptures or comments shared with me during my lifetime that have motivated me to "keep it moving." I pray they will help you as well.

✧

"Not going back, I'm moving ahead, I'm here to declare to you, my past is over, In You, all things are made new, surrendered my life to Christ, I'm moving, moving forward."

~ ISRAEL HOUGHTON ~

"Life's Little Lessons - GOOD, bad, or InDiFfErEnT
That Get You from Here to There"

My Thoughts Quotes and Questions	Scriptures	Other	Miscellaneous
Why do men and women cheat?	"Whoso findeth a wife findeth a good thing, And obtaineth favor of Jehovah." Prov 18:22	If a man is interested He'll let you know.- Nadine King	That gives me pause.- Tyler Perry, The Family that Preys
If you're unhappy, why are you still in that relationship?	"Wives, be in subjection unto your own husbands, as unto the Lord." Eph 5:22	You're here and you're trying to get there and the "T" that makes "here," there are the tests, trials, or tribulations you must go through to get there. Chester D. T. Baldwin	The enemy is anything that hinders the purpose of God in your life. Pastor Jesse Curney III
When someone says, "You give me that wow factor," what they're really saying is: "I enjoy having sex with you."	"Husbands, love your wives, even as Christ also loved the church, and gave himself up for it." Eph 5:25	You can only claim what God told you, you could have.- Pastor Jesse Curney III	What good is it to appreciate what God gives us if we don't appreciate the giver of the gift? T. D. Jakes
If you're not happy in a relationship or situation, don't tarry.	Today, God's Word can heal your yesterdays. "Jesus Christ is the same yesterday and to-day, yea and for ever." Heb 13:8	If you don't believe that God won't do it, then just ask!- Michael M. Knight	It's nothing worth adverting something you're fresh out of T. D. Jakes
Have you ever asked yourself, "Why Me? Then God responds, "Why not you?"	"For I know the plans I have for you," declares the LORD, "plans to prosper you and not to harm you, plans to give you hope and a future." Jer. 29:11 (NIV)	Whatever place God brings you to, He makes provision for you there.	You've already taken all my stuff. What more do I have to give or what more do you want from me? For Colored Girls
It's all for His glory!	Man plans but God directs!!! A man's goings are established of Jehovah; And he delighteth in his way." Ps 37:23	I didn't think he was your type. What's my type?- Dana Holmes	They've been doing that all their lives. About me and my family. A way of living; A lifestyle. Kenneth L. Brown
God blesses the effort.	"Wisdom is the principal thing; therefore get wisdom; Yea, with all thy getting get understanding." Prov 4:7	The two of you are too strong willed. It will never work.- An "outsider" looking in on my marriage 1997-2007	It's the will of the man, not the skill of the man. Denzel Washington, He Got Game
It's not about where you are, but always about where you are going.	Being fully persuaded that He will do what He promised. Rom 4:21	How high is your mountain? Not too high that you can't climb with God. –Pastor A.W. Anthony Mays	Re-think that thing you're thinking to do; don't wait until it's conceived. Kenneth Morris

"Life's Little Lessons - GOOD, bad, or InDiFfErEnT That Get You from Here to There"

In a relationship, you must be present.	"…As the Father gave me commandment, even so I do…" John 14:31	Do you have the mental fortitude to hang with me? JCE III	Can't see the forest for the trees. Unknown
God can fix any problem. However, you must first give it to Him.	"…Not by might, nor by power, but by my Spirit, saith Jehovah of hosts." Zech 4:6	Never do evil for evil.- Jesse Mae Walker	It's a new season, it's a new day.-Israel & New Breed, Season
First the Test, then the Testimony-can't have the testimony without the test.	We act upon what we think about (previews of coming attractions). "Let the words of my mouth and the meditation of my heart Be acceptable in thy sight, O Jehovah, my rock, and my redeemer." Ps 19:14	God doesn't hide from us, we hide from him, but not as though he was hiding. He doesn't play Hide-and-Seek.- T.D. Jakes	Do things other people won't do and you will have things other people won't have!
Trust God to strengthen and grant you peace, while He makes the necessary adjustments in your life-it's for His glory.	Watch what you allow to plug into and draw strength from you. Gen 2:21-22	Stop fighting battles that God hasn't called you to.- Dana Holmes	A man doesn't make excuses.-Alfred Kitchens Jr.
You don't have to stand up tall, but you do have to stand up.	Who knows what God will produce if we go all out for him?- All Points Bulletin Ask, Seek & Knock Matt 7:7-8	Common practice becomes law. JCE III	The devil can only take what you give him, and what he wants is what you give to God. Pastor Jesse Curney III
You're using your emotions without the benefit of intellect.	A man reaps what he sows. Gal 6:7	Who are you and where did you come from?- LP	God won't give you anything you haven't pursued.
The same thing that makes you laugh is the same thing that makes you cry.	"But thanks be unto God, who always leadeth us in triumph in Christ…" 2 Cor 2:14	Because God loves you, He will stay in a house that's not fully cleaned.- T.D. Jakes	When you are where you belong, no one can compete. Blessings wait for you there.
We are "WUC"- Women Under Construction; A product built by God.	Things covered will not heal well. "I shall not die, but live, And declare the works of Jehovah." Ps 118:17	You are who you are because of your story. You're history.- T.D. Jakes	Your mind needs an example to follow. Follow me as I follow Christ (1 Cor 11:1).
God has to minister to you, before you can begin to minister to someone else.	"Behold, I go forward, but he is not there; And backward, but I cannot perceive him; On the left hand, when he doth work, but I cannot behold him; He hideth himself on the right hand, that I cannot see him." Job 23:8-9	Just like in sports, you got to keep playing until the whistle blows. Don't give up too soon because of what it looks like. Don't abort the process before you get the blessing or lesson God has in store for you. You will win, in Jesus' name.- Pastor Jesse Curney III	Happy moments, Praise God. Difficult moments, Seek God. Quiet moments, Worship God. Painful moments, Trust God. Every moment, Thank God!-Rick Warren

"Life's Little Lessons - GOOD, bad, or InDiFfErEnT
That Get You from Here to There"

A chart has been provided for you to list those thoughts, quotes, scriptures or other comments that can help you move forward positively.

My Thoughts Quotes and Questions	Scriptures	Other	Miscellaneous

Chapter Three

Real Life Situations

That Get You From Here To There

Part I

Husbands should love their wives as Christ loves the church

Wives, submit yourselves unto your own husbands as to God

Children, obey your parents in the Lord, for this is right

A family that prays together stays together.

HUSBAND AND WIFE STUFF
"Nuff Sed"

SITUATION: You're married and things aren't going well in your relationship. You are both sleeping in separate rooms. You want to make love to your spouse badly, but know you will be rejected by him. What do you do?

THOUGHT: When we (as women) feel unwanted, it destroys our self-esteem. God Himself, has a way of touching you like none other. Pray, relax and know that you are loved and wanted by God. Sex should not be withheld from one another in marriage, as that opens the door for the enemy to come in and wreak havoc. When this happens, some women might feel as Tamar did when she was raped by her half-brother, Amnon, saying, "...Sending me away now is worse than what you've already done to me,".   2 SAM 13:16, NLT

How Would You Handle It?

_____

_____

_____

_____

What Does God's Word Say About it?

Let the husband render unto the wife her due: and likewise also the wife unto the husband. The wife hath not power over her own body, but the husband: and likewise also the husband hath not power over his own body, but the wife. Defraud ye not one the other, except it be by consent for a season, that ye may give yourselves unto prayer, and may be together again, that Satan tempt you not because of your incontinency. I CORINTHIANS 7:3-5

SITUATION: Your husband always has to under the influence before he can make love to you.

THOUGHT: Sounds like he's just not that in to you, if he needs a buzz to put him in the mood to make love to you. Maybe you're not the woman for him, mentally. Every man isn't for every woman and every woman isn't for every man. I'm almost sure this was probably happening before you got married, and nothing was done to address it then, now it's become a problem in your marriage. Have a discussion with your spouse to determine the reason for him having to be high to be with you, as the issue might be resolved just by talking it over with him. Ever thought about that? I would recommend that the two of you seek counseling to assist him with getting "there" physically, mentally or emotionally-it's called "Save-a-Marriage."

How Would You Handle It?

_____

_____

_____

_____

What Does God's Word Say About it?

Let thy fountain be blessed; And rejoice in the wife of thy youth. As a loving hind and a pleasant doe, Let her breasts satisfy thee at all times; And be thou ravished always with her love. PROVERBS 5:18-19

SITUATION: Your spouse has just come home and informed you that he had an affair. In telling you about his unfaithfulness, he feels that you should just accept the fact that he cheated and confessed, and move forward with no more talk of the incident.

THOUGHT: Who does that? In the real world that doesn't happen. A person first needs time to heal and grieve such an unthinkable act. We forgive, but we don't forget. It takes time to heal and trust the offender again. You better be glad she didn't go out and bust the windows out of your car! SMH! I'm not advocating violence here, but that's what most women would have done, if not more.

How Would You Handle It?

_____

_____

_____

_____

What Does God's Word Say About It?

*Whoever commits adultery with a woman lacks understanding; He
who does so destroys his own soul .*   PROVERBS 6:32 (NKJV)

—m—

SITUATION: You're upset because your husband didn't wake you up for church and then decides to go without you. He gets upset because you choose to go out and celebrate your daughter's birthday and don't get home until after 2:00 a.m. He says you are disrespecting the marriage, and you say he's wrong for not waking you up to go to church.

THOUGHT: Wow! You're both wrong-the marriage should be important enough to both of you that you communicate with one another on a better level. The Word says that you should leave and cleave (Gen 2:24), and nothing or no one should come between the two of you. Nothing beats communication; especially in marriage-it is a must. Be honest with yourself. Stop the finger-pointing amongst the two of you and talk to one another. If that doesn't help, you should seek counseling. Somewhere in our minds we seem to think that going to counseling is a bad thing. News alert: it's the best thing that you can do for yourself and your marriage. Stay home sometimes and work on your marriage. Now, dat oughta holja!

How Would You Handle It?

_____

_____

_____

_____

What Does God's Word Say About It?

Therefore shall a man leave his father and his mother, and shall cleave unto his wife: and they shall be one flesh. GENESIS 2:24

Shall two walk together, except they have agreed? AMOS 3:3

And if thy right hand causeth thee to stumble, cut it off, and cast it from thee: for it is profitable for thee that one of thy members should perish, and not thy whole body go into hell. MATTHEW 5:30

—m—

SITUATION: Your spouse is angry and separates from you because he wants a new car. He goes to the credit union to negotiate, only to find out that he's behind on his car note. Your spouse has a selfish tendency to want to do certain things, which take away from the finances. Because you refuse to address the issue, it presents a financial hardship for the two of you. He leaves you and runs right into the arms of another woman who provides the finances he needs to get him caught up. Months later, he does get that new car and the two of you eventually reconcile.

THOUGHT: Stop robbing Peter to pay Paul and start living within your means. Your husband needs to know that he can't buy or get everything that he wants when there are other bills that need immediate attention. As his help meet, you should communicate when the finances are in the "red." Seeking financial advice would be a good option. The best option would be tithing, if that's not already being done. As for the separation, that was something that he wanted to do anyway. If it was that easy for another woman to come in, waving her money around and he following it like a dog in heat, there must have been some underlying marital issues. Check yourself before you wreck yourself.

How Would You Handle It?

_____

_____

_____

_____

What Does God's Word Say About It?

> *Bring ye the whole tithe into the store-house, that there may be food in my house, and prove me now herewith, saith Jehovah of hosts,*

if I will not open you the windows of heaven, and pour you out a blessing, that there shall not be room enough to receive it.
MALACHI 3:10

And he said, That which proceedeth out of the man, that defileth the man. For from within, out of the heart of men, evil thoughts proceed, fornications, thefts, murders, adulteries, covetings, wickednesses, deceit, lasciviousness, an evil eye, railing, pride, foolishness.
MARK 7:20-22

—⚇—

SITUATION: You marry your first love (your everything), have two beautiful children and think your marriage is going to last forever. You find out that your husband is selfish, egotistical and verbally abusive, which takes a toll on your family. Not to mention, the multiple affairs and constant assaults on your psyche and the strain that it puts on the children over the years. As they have gotten older, they simply just tolerate their father's behavior or have no desire to have a relationship with him. You finally decide to leave.

THOUGHT: Sounds like grounds for divorce. You did the right thing my sistah, by leaving and getting your children out of that unsafe place and seeking refuge. Everyone has to evaluate the "shelf life" of their relationships from time to time. Some are perishable, and will go bad if neglected or abused. It's so important to know the shelf life of everyone we come in contact with so that we know for certain, when it's time to clean up and take out the trash. In regards to the children, they may want or need a relationship with their father as they grow older. It should be up to them to reach out to their father, if they so desire.

How Would You Handle It?

_____

_____

_____

_____

What Does God's Word Say About It?

> *And we know that to them that love God all things work together for good, even to them that are called according to his purpose.*
> ROMANS 8:28

> *Children, obey your parents in the Lord: for this is right. Honor thy father and mother (which is the first commandment with promise), that it may be well with thee, and thou mayest live long on the earth. And, ye fathers, provoke not your children to wrath: but nurture them in the chastening and admonition of the Lord.*
> EPHESIANS 6:1-4

—⚌—

SITUATION: You marry the man of your dreams; the one that loves you unconditionally; the one that will do anything for you. The two of you make plans to move to a larger city/state for better job opportunities. Your husband's plan is to go to school, start a business and have you join him once all is complete. Everything goes as planned. He completes school, opens up the business, and even finds and purchases the house you desire. However, something happens and you choose not to come as planned. You begin making excuses for not visiting regularly. You wait just a little too long, allowing the enemy to slip into the crack you left open. Because your husband is lonely, he strikes up a relationship with an old flame. She begins to fill the empty time and space. Your husband begins to lose trust in you because of the loss of time and the excuses. You speak to each other, but things just aren't the same. When you finally realize what is happening, he has already filed for divorce and made plans to start a new life with the other woman.

THOUGHT: Now this is a serious and personal thing and you and only you, know why you didn't follow the plan, why you made excuses, why you just didn't make that move. You are responsible for what happened in your marriage. You really can't blame anyone else, unless there were pre-existing issues that were never addressed. It is so important to keep those lines of communication open, especially when there's distance between the two of you. Sometimes absence makes the heart grow fonder, sometimes it doesn't. You should never let a relationship get to the point of no return, especially in marriage. There's always another way to handle a situation before it gets out of hand, but you have to open up your mouth and talk. Nothing beats communication and understanding-nothing. You owe it to yourself, your spouse, and to the marriage to at least try before you throw in the towel or make a decision that you'll both regret. It takes two;

one can never do it alone. You both are equally responsible for the marriage and the vows you made to one another and to God. The Word says that the two shall become one.

How Would You Handle It?

_____

_____

_____

_____

What Does God's Word Say About It?

For where two or three are gathered together in my name, there am I in the midst of them. MATTHEW 18:20

Love suffereth long, and is kind; love envieth not; love vaunteth not itself, is not puffed up, doth not behave itself unseemly, seeketh not its own, is not provoked, taketh not account of evil; rejoiceth not in unrighteousness, but rejoiceth with the truth; beareth all things, believeth all things, hopeth all things, endureth all things.

I CORINTHIANS 13:4-7

SITUATION: You're married and your husband has some concerns with your physical appearance, as you're no runway model. You're a little hairy, and a little overweight, but you're always presentable. Instead of him discussing it with you, he confides in his Aunt, who doesn't particularly care for you because you don't meet her standards of the type of woman she feels her nephew should be married to. He tells you after the fact, and realizes that he made a big mistake in confiding in his Aunt and not discussing his concerns with you to begin with. He actually gets mad at some of the things his Aunt says. To make it up to you, he buys you perfume, nice lingerie, and expresses that he would prefer that you shave your legs regularly, and that the two of you begin working out together.

THOUGHT: Ok, did he not ask you to be his wife, and did he not know that you had those personal features before he married you? Ugh! Well, I'm glad to see that he used a softer approach to the situation by finally coming to discuss this problem with you, and bearing gifts, I might add. In marriage, it's never a good thing to discuss issues or concerns with family members, before coming to your spouse and discussing them. Family members are always going to be biased towards their own-that's natural. Who you choose to be with has nothing to do with your family. The Bible says that you "leave and cleave," which means the two shall become one flesh, united in attitude, mind, vision and direction. Never allow outsiders to dictate what you do or how you manage your marriage. The two of you (hopefully) should've worked out all those kinks before you said "I do." The way your family sees it, nobody's ever good enough for you, which is good, but you have to live your own life and not through their eyes. If you don't, you'll never be happy and your family will always have the control-hold over your life. You'll probably end up resenting them for a decision you made, based on advice they offered.

How Would You Handle It?

_____

_____

_____

_____

What Does God's Word Say About It?

> *And Ruth said, Entreat me not to leave thee, and to return from
> following after thee, for whither thou goest, I will go; and where
> thou lodgest, I will lodge; thy people shall be my people, and thy God
> my God.*   RUTH 1:16

—⟐—

SITUATION: You're married now, but once dated a local celebrity.
Over a holiday weekend while he is performing in your city, he asks
to meet your husband and would like for you to meet his wife. You
arrange for the meeting to take place. The introductions go well; as
you already advised your husband that this is a person you once
dated. Time passes and it gets late. Your ex-lover decides not to get
on the road and travel back home. He and his wife try getting a hotel,
but due to the late hour and the holiday, they can't find a room. Your
husband offers to have them stay as your house guests. They accept
the invitation and it seems a little strange to have your ex-lover and
your husband under the same roof. Your ex-lover is actually happy

for you and when you have a moment alone; he expresses that he still and will always have feelings for you. Awkward!

THOUGHT: Stranger things have probably happened, but to be under the same roof with your husband and ex-lover is kind of weird. What must be going through yours, yours husband's and your ex-lover's minds has to be crazy thoughts. You are probably wondering, "How did I get myself into this mess?" How uncomfortable it must be. You most likely have thoughts about when you and your ex were together. The fact that he mentioned that he still has feelings for you simply didn't help matters at all. You have to take your mind off the past and focus on the present. God has a way of making all things plain and clear. He sets the stage for exes and new spouses to meet and to be comfortable with being in the same place, even after they have been with the same person. There's no explanation for that, except that God does all things well (Mk 7:37). You really have to move on mentally and physically.

How Would You Handle It?

_____

_____

_____

_____

What Does God's Word Say About It?

And I saw a new heaven and a new earth; for the first heaven and the first earth are passed away; and the sea is no more. And I saw the holy city, new Jerusalem, coming down out of heaven of God, made ready as a bride adorned for her husband. And I heard a great

voice out of the throne saying, Behold, the tabernacle of God is with
men, and he shall dwell with them, and they shall be his peoples,
and God himself shall be with them, and be their God: and he shall
wipe away every tear from their eyes; and death shall be no more;
neither shall there be mourning, nor crying, nor pain, any more: the
first things are passed away. And he that sitteth on the throne said,
Behold, I make all things new. And he saith, Write: for these words
are faithful and true. REVELATION 21:1-5

SITUATION: You are very unhappy in your marriage. Your spouse doesn't satisfy you physically, mentally or emotionally, anymore. You don't like the fact that he doesn't trust you as far as he can throw you. He buys you any and everything that glitters to cover up the insecurities he has from being cheated on in past relationships. You dread coming home when you know he's going to be there. You have talked to him concerning this issue until you're blue in the face. He expresses that he's going to get help, as he doesn't want to lose you, but doesn't take the necessary steps to do so because he doesn't feel he really has a problem. The two of you begin to operate as roommates, and all that glitters now rests in an empty room, occupied only by your spouse.

THOUGHT: Why does this subject come up more and more in marriage? Why is it that the enemy is running so rampant in relationships that are supposed to be sounder, more together, and more connected? Is it because we are not interviewing and spending time to get to know the persons we are connecting with in marriage? Then we get married and find out that the person we married is not who we thought they were. At that point, it's already too late. The first thing we want to do is go to divorce court and get out of the marriage as fast as we can, when what we really need to do is go back to basics and stop, look and listen to our hearts. Just because a person treats you well doesn't mean he or she is the person you should spend the rest of your life with. What about compatibility, love, respect and companionship-all those other things that contribute to a marriage? Most importantly, what about God? He definitely needs to be in the mix for your marriage to work. Here's the equation for a good marriage: God + Man + Woman = One. For an even balance, you need to add the following ingredients: Communication, Honesty, Understanding, Commitment, and Team Effort. God is the only one who can take a wrong and turn it around for your good. He alone, has the solution to all of your problems.

How Would You Handle It?

_____

_____

_____

_____

What Does God's Word Say About It?

> *And it shall come to pass, if thou shalt hearken diligently unto the voice of Jehovah thy God, to observe to do all his commandments which I command thee this day, that Jehovah thy God will set thee on high above all the nations of the earth: and all these blessings shall come upon thee, and overtake thee, if thou shalt hearken unto*

the voice of Jehovah thy God. Blessed shalt thou be in the city, and blessed shalt thou be in the field. Blessed shall be the fruit of thy body, and the fruit of thy ground, and the fruit of thy beasts, the increase of thy cattle, and the young of thy flock. Blessed shall be thy basket and thy kneading-trough. DEUTERONOMY 28:1-5

SITUATION: You are a married woman, in an unhappy situation. You meet a divorced man at a work-related event. The two of you have seen one another on a few occasions because of the nature of your work. You converse and find out that you actually have a lot in common. He makes you feel good by paying you compliments and recognizes who you are and what you're about (what a bonus that is!). Outside of company events, you only talk over the phone. There are no private meetings at this point because you are still married, and unwilling to take a chance on being in this man's presence alone. Some part of you feels guilty for holding these types of conversations over the phone, as it feels like you are cheating on your spouse, who you are having no relations with at the present time.

THOUGHT: I'm sure the reward is that this man met you-whether you go forward in a relationship or not. However, in marriage you must always be careful not to cross that invisible line and get caught up. You don't even have the right to look at another man other than your husband (Matt 5:28). You should keep your friendship with this man strictly platonic, at least until you are divorced. If it's meant to be, it'll be. If he feels you are the basic reward now, then you'll be the Academy Award once you're single and free. Then you'll be able to spend some real time getting to know him. Don't spoil what could be a wonderful, lasting relationship later for the apparent urgency of the present.

How Would You Handle It?

_____

_____

_____

_____

What Does God's Word Say About It?

> For the woman that hath a husband is bound by law to the husband
> while he liveth; but if the husband die, she is discharged from the law
> of the husband. ROMANS 7:2

—⟶w⟵—

SITUATION: Your husband comes in on a Saturday evening and announces that he has nothing else to do so he'll take you out for a burger. It makes you feel as though if something else had come up, then the dinner wouldn't have been a thought. Then, he insists that you review the menu before you get to the restaurant because he doesn't like when you ask questions regarding the food because it embarrasses him. As you review the menu, trying to locate a certain burger, he begins to harass you by saying, "You're not reading the menu." You state that you are indeed looking at the menu but he insists that you are not, to the point that you feel like he is trying to pick an argument to prevent the outing. Next, your husband tells you not to ask any questions when you arrive at the restaurant. He is angry and you don't understand why nor do you want to set him off. As you begin to place your order, you ask the waiter to add lettuce and tomatoes to your burger and you inquire about how hot the sauce is. Your husband interrupts and says, "That's why I told you to read the menu before we got here." He rolls his eyes and shakes his head. As you ask the waiter for lemonade, your husband asks, "Was it on the menu?" You respond "No." He retorts, "Then they don't have it." The waiter confirms they do have lemonade." On your way to your seat your husband makes the following comment: "I'm trying to make you better. Every time we go out to eat, you always have to ask about the food. It's embarrassing and you irritate the waiter. You think you're so perfect and never do anything wrong."

THOUGHT: Oh, I know this behavior all too well. It looks like he's trying to make excuses so he can go be with someone else, or perhaps he would much rather be doing something else. It all started when he said that he would take you out for a burger, because he didn't have anything else to do. That's when I would have said, "Thanks, but no thanks!" It appears that your husband was trying his best to not take you out at all. Sometimes all the proof we need is right before our very eyes, but we refuse to see or accept it. One thing I can say about a man is that he says what he means, and means what he says; we simply don't listen.

Insulting a person is never a way of making them better. Correction or criticism should be done in love, as that is what conquers all. Did he know you were asking questions regarding the food because you were watching your weight? It seems he didn't even consider that. Know this one thing: he's the one with an issue, not you.

How Would You Handle It?

_____

_____

_____

_____

What Does God's Word Say About It?

Bless are ye when men shall reproach you, and persecute you, and say all manner of evil against you falsely, for my sake. Rejoice, and be exceeding glad: for great is your reward in heaven: for so persecuted they the prophets that were before you. MATTHEW 5:11-12

Let no man therefore judge you in mean, or in drink, or in respect of a feast day or a new moon or a sabbath day. COLOSSIANS 2:16

—⁂—

SITUATION: Your husband has the responsibility of taking care of the finances in your household. From time to time, he goes on spending sprees, buying things that are not needed. He is not cognizant of the important bills that must be paid and the amount he's spending which causes you to end up in the "red." During a critical time when you are trying to upgrade your living arrangements and waiting to be approved, he goes on a spending spree and doesn't exactly tell you about it. The necessary funds are not available, which causes you to not be able to move as originally planned. You are so upset at him for being irresponsible. This destroys your trust in his ability to handle the finances, as he's done this many times before. After discussing the issue, you take away his privileges of writing checks, using his ATM or credit cards, and you are now handling the finances until you can trust him again. However, you are happy that your husband acknowledges that his pride got in the way, as he didn't want to admit that he couldn't handle the finances on his own.

THOUGHT: In most marriages the finances are handled by the person who knows how to manage money well. Personally, I think the finances should be discussed among both partners and handled by the one who is most responsible. Finances are one of the major reasons why many marriages end in divorce. Someone always spends more or wants more than the other spouse, when there should be discussion concerning how the money is spent and delegated. Managing the finances should be a joint venture. The Word says that the two become one. This should be in everything you do in marriage. Even in your finances, you both should know what's happening at all times. You should be on the same page. Being accountable to one another is so important in marriage. Discussing finances before marriage should help you to decide how they will be handled during your marriage, and who will be responsible for them. Someone once said, "Allow a boy to grow and he will come back a man; be with a boy who needs to grow and he will grow up to be a tall boy rather than a sound man." Steve Harvey recommends that couples should have four accounts: one for household bills, a savings account, and individual accounts for each spouse; that way you always know where everything is going.

How Would You Handle It?

_____

_____

_____

_____

What Does God's Word Say About It?

For the love of money is a root of all kinds of evil: which some reaching after have been led astray from the faith, and have pierced themselves through with many sorrows. 1 TIMOTHY 6:10

There is that scattereth, and increaseth yet more; And there is that withholdeth more than is meet, but it tendeth only to want. The liberal soul shall be made fat; And he that watereth shall be watered also himself. PROVERBS 11:24-25

—⚬—

SITUATION: Your husband has come home on many occasions and informed you that the fellows on his job pass pornography around like it's nothing. They discuss sex all day, talk about cheating and are always trying to get him to go out to the strip club. Your husband is working the late shift one night and gives you a call. You hear Snoop Dogg's Drop It Like It's Hot record in the background and wonder if your husband has finally given in to the fellows. You're glad when you find out that the song is his co-worker's ringtone. That doesn't mean you think he would never do any of the things his co-workers do. However, you would be wrong to assume he could not continue to stand strong in the midst of a negative work environment.

THOUGHT: I believe that many times men discuss or do these types of things at work because they are not comfortable or don't have time to do them at home. It doesn't mean that they don't have the desire to do them. Like many other women, you would probably be concerned that your husband could possibly be out with the fellows, exposing himself to other women, all because of a simple phone call that sent your mind into overload. Although you know your husband very well, there may have been a small possibility in the back of your mind that he was out doing something he wasn't supposed to be doing. Be sure to communicate with your husband instead of accusing him of being unfaithful. Hey ladies, all men are not out cheating. Sometimes, we just have to ask the right questions to get the answers we're looking for.

How Would You Handle It?

_____

_____

_____

_____

What Does God's Word Say About It?

For as he thinketh within himself, so is he: Eat and drink, saith he to thee; But his heart is not with thee. PROVERB 23:7

FAMILY MATTERS

SITUATION: Your spouse either refuses or says he cannot do what is necessary to safeguard his health; ignoring doctor's orders, pleas from loved ones, common sense, and insists it's his life. The daily decisions he makes are self-centered, and unbelievably unloving toward you. He is making unilateral decisions that affect the quality of your life, just as much as his. If you stay in the relationship, you are forced to slide down that razor blade with him.

THOUGHT: It's very selfish to not consider those who love and want to keep you around when you are battling a disease, serious health condition, or illness. We need one another to survive. When you find someone who can love you in spite of your ailments, you are blessed. God loves with an everlasting love. I wonder what would happen if we loved like He loves. Your life is not your own-it belongs to God and should be shared with the ones who love you. Choose to live and love those you are connected to daily, no matter the condition or situation. You hurt the ones who love you most when you try to make it on your own, without their help. If your loved one's recklessness is putting you in harm's way, you need to remove yourself from that place and seek protection. You may need counseling for any emotional suffering that has occurred. Remember your vows: "Do you promise to love, comfort, honor and keep him/her for better or worse, for richer or poorer, in sickness and health, and forsaking all others, be faithful only to him/her, for as long as you both shall live? I'm sure you both said, "I do."

How Would You Handle It?

_____

_____

_____

_____

What Does God's Word Say About It?

> *But God commendeth his own love toward us, in that, while we were yet sinners, Christ died for us.* ROMANS 5:8

> *But the things which proceed out of the mouth come forth out of the heart; and they defile the man. For out of the heart come forth evil thoughts, murders, adulteries, fornications, thefts, false witness, railings.* MATTHEW 15:18-19

PARENTING

SITUATION: Your young adult daughter's male friend comes to your house at midnight to see her. This is the second time he has done this.

THOUGHT: This is a no-no! Either he's married or getting off from work at that time of the morning. Either way, he would have one more time to do it before he gets the ax. You should let your daughter handle the situation before you do, as this man is disrespecting her and her household. No respectable man would do this. Does he not know or remember the "Golden Rule?"

How Would You Handle It?

_____

_____

_____

_____

What Does God's Word Say About It?

All things therefore whatsoever ye would that men should do unto you, even so do ye also unto them: for this is the law and the prophets.
MATTHEW 7:12

And as ye would that men should do to you, do ye also to them likewise. LUKE 6:31

SITUATION: You're dating a guy who you think is great. He's caring, kind and considerate. There is one problem: he has a child with another woman, who always puts the child at risk and doesn't really want to have anything to do with the child, unless he is involved. You communicated to him many times that he needs to deal with the interfering baby's mama, but he doesn't do anything about her or her meddling ways. When you decide to tell him that you would prefer that he handles the situation with his baby's mama to prevent any problems in the future for the two of you, he gets angry and begins harassing you about not wanting to be with him and accuses you of having an affair.

THOUGHT: Red flag! It's better that you experience this behavior before you get too involved with this person and the "Baby Mama Drama." He should be handling his affairs better as it relates to his child and baby's mama. It shouldn't be your problem or spill over into your relationship. Although we inherit some of the problems of the person we choose to date, especially when there's a child involved (it's called "Baby Mama Drama" all day everyday and twice on Sunday's), that's for him to handle-not you. This would be a direct indication of how he handles his business. If he doesn't handle this well, there's a possibility he won't handle other problems between the two of you well.

How Would You Handle It?

_____

_____

_____

_____

What Does God's Word Say About It?

Be not deceived: Evil companionships corrupt good morals.
1 CORINTHIANS 15:33

Part II

"Oh, I say and I say it again,

Ya been had!

Ya been took!

Ya been hoodwinked!

Bamboozled!

Led astray!

Run amok!

This is what He does..

DATING MISHAPS

SITUATION: You're in an uncommitted relationship and your significant other tells you that he has decided to go back to his ex-wife, but also tells you he's falling in love with you. Then he asks what you think he should do.

THOUGHT: Wow! I'm gone need a minute. Actually, you probably already know what you're going to do. You just need someone to validate your decision. No one can really tell you what to do. However, you should pray about the situation and follow your heart. What's in your heart is how you really feel and how you should most likely respond. Once the decision is made, stick with your decision and move on.

How Would You Handle It?

_____

_____

_____

_____

What Does God's Word Say About It?

> *I will bless Jehovah, who hath given me counsel; Yea, my heart instructeth me in the night seasons.* PSALM 16:7

> *My beloved put in his hand by the hole of the door, And my heart was moved for him.* SONG OF SOLOMON 5:4

Blessed are the pure in heart: for they shall see God. MATTHEW 5:8

For where thy treasure is, there will thy heart be also. MATTHEW 6:21

SITUATION: There is a man who says he wants to be with you, but is already in a relationship with someone else. He is making a conscious effort to see you whenever he can. You ask why he's still in the relationship if he doesn't want to be there. He says that it's not by choice.

THOUGHT: Excuse me! It is by choice and he made the decision to be with another person instead of with you. People always have a choice. To thine own self be true. If this man made a choice to be with someone else, then you should accept his decision and move forward. Choose what happens to you daily-don't allow someone else to.

How Would You Handle It?

_____

_____

_____

_____

What Does God's Word Say About It?

> *And ye shall know the truth, and the truth shall make you free.*
> JOHN 8:32

For freedom did Christ set us free: stand fast therefore, and be not entangled again in a yoke of bondage. GALATIANS 5:1

For the law of the Spirit of life in Christ Jesus made me free from the law of sin and of death. ROMANS 8:2

— m —

SITUATION: You go out on a first date with a particular man. Afterwards, the two of you go back to his house and have sex.

THOUGHT: You got me drunk, took advantage of me and I liked it. Wrong answer. It's never a good decision to get physical with a man immediately after meeting him. You rob yourself of the opportunity of getting to know him. This causes so many problems-you don't even have a clue as to what you're getting yourself into. What about the mental and emotional aspects of the relationship? Because of the physical attraction in many cases, you won't be able to "see the forest for the trees." You also risk losing respect after the act, and the possibility of not seeing this man again. Don't do it, don't do it!

How Would You Handle It?

_____

_____

_____

_____

What Does God's Word Say About It?

Now the works of the flesh are manifest, which are [these]: fornication, uncleanness, lasciviousness, idolatry, sorcery, enmities, strife, jealousies, wraths, factions, divisions, parties, envyings, drunkenness, revellings, and such like; of which I forewarn you, even as I did forewarn you, that they who practise such things shall not inherit the kingdom of God. GALATIANS 5:19-21

Wherefore God gave them up in the lusts of their hearts unto uncleanness, that their bodies should be dishonored among themselves: For this cause God gave them up unto vile passions: for their women changed the natural use into that which is against nature: and likewise also the men, leaving the natural use of the woman, burned in their lust one toward another, men with men working unseemliness, and receiving in themselves that recompense of their error which was due.   And even as they refused to have God in their knowledge, God gave them up unto a reprobate mind, to do those things which are not fitting; being filled with all unrighteousness, wickedness, covetousness, maliciousness; full of envy, murder, strife, deceit, malignity; whisperers, ROMANS 1:24, 26-29

SITUATION: A man whom you were involved with goes back to his ex-wife but realizes that he's still unhappy with her. He stays in the relationship but makes it a point to let you know that he hasn't re-married her yet.

THOUGHT: ROTFLOL! Now, why would it be important to the person you left for your ex-wife, to know that you haven't re-married? If he's unhappy in the situation, he shouldn't tarry. The person he left is still the same person. People don't actually change; their situation changes, which alters their perspective. Life's too short for him to waste his time being in a place or with a person that he doesn't really want to be with. Here's some food for thought for this man: Why return to your ex-wife and live as a married couple if you don't intend to actually re-marry her? Why would you settle for plain and simple when you can wait and get what you really want (if he actually knows what that is)? As for you, why be "Plan B" when you could be someone else's first choice?

How Would You Handle It?

_____

_____

_____

_____

What Does God's Word Say About It?

> *Jesus Christ is the same yesterday and to-day, yea and for ever.*
> HEBREWS 13:8
>
> *For I, Jehovah, change not; therefore ye, O sons of Jacob, are not consumed.* MALACHI 3:6
>
> *God is not a man, that he should lie, Neither the son of man, that he should repent: Hath he said, and will he not do it? Or hath he spoken, and will he not make it good?* NUMBERS 23:19

But if they have not continency, let them marry: for it is better to marry than to burn. I CORINTHIANS 7:9

———————————— —₥— ————————————

SITUATION: You are in a relationship with a very nice guy. He has all the qualities that you are seeking. He's a gentleman, he loves the Lord, he's a hard-working man who will provide for you and understands the principles of taking care of his woman. However, he doesn't satisfy you sexually-ouch!

THOUGHT: As women, we seek many things in a man. We like them handsome, strong, gainfully employed, etc. Most importantly, we want them to be able to satisfy us sexually. If things are not well in the sexual department, there will eventually be a problem. Men are visual and women are emotional. Just the mere thought that your mate is not able to satisfy you is an immediate turn-off. It doesn't matter how fine he is or what he does. If the main tools are not working, there will be troubles in paradise. Be honest with this guy and let him know that it's not working for you. Inform him that if you continue to see one another, you will need to work on this issue together. It would be helpful for you to communicate what it would take to satisfy you.

How Would You Handle It?

———————————————————————————
———————————————————————————
———————————————————————————
———————————————————————————

What Does God's Word Say About It?

*Ye have heard that it was said, Thou shalt not commit adultery:
but I say unto you, that every one that looketh on a woman to lust
after her hath committed adultery with her already in his heart. And
if thy right eye causeth thee to stumble, pluck it out, and cast it
from thee: for it is profitable for thee that one of thy members should
perish, and not thy whole body be cast into hell. And if thy right
hand causeth thee to stumble, cut it off, and cast it from thee: for it
is profitable for thee that one of thy members should perish, and not
thy whole body go into hell.*   MATTHEW 5:27-30*

*Let marriage be had in honor among all, and let the bed be undefiled:
for fornicators and adulterers God will judge.*   HEBREWS 13:4

—⧖—

SITUATION: You are in a new relationship with a decent guy. He has
expressed that he is committed to being with you exclusively. Things are
going well, when an old flame starts calling, asking to see you again. He
is in a relationship but expresses how much he misses you and how good
he felt when the two of you were together. You have to admit that the sex
was real good when you were with him. What do you do?

THOUGHT: Ok, enquiring minds want to know why he left to begin
with if he was feeling you like that. He can't have his cake and eat it,
too. What triggered him to suddenly come back into your life? It sounds
like he's not good at making decisions or that he made the wrong one.

You should let him know that you are honored that he has expressed his feelings, but you have moved on with someone who really wants to be in a relationship with you. It's not your fault that he ran the risk of you not wanting to get back with him after he realized what he had. It would be hard for you to trust that he wouldn't make the same mistake again. Finally, if sex is the factor that you're basing your decision on, you might want to re-think it. You really need to focus and determine what's important to you. I wouldn't give that old flame one minute of my time or even think of rekindling anything with him. It's a shame that it took him too long to recognize that you were the right choice all along. If you snooze, you lose!

How Would You Handle It?

_____

_____

_____

_____

What Does God's Word Say About It?

> The plans of the heart belong to man; But the answer of the tongue is from Jehovah. All the ways of a man are clean in his own eyes; But Jehovah weigheth the spirits. Commit thy works unto Jehovah, And thy purposes shall be established. Jehovah hath made everything for its own end; Yea, even the wicked for the day of evil. Every one that is proud in heart is an abomination to Jehovah: Though hand join in hand, he shall not be unpunished. PROVERBS 16:1-5

* For additional understanding read the entire chapter.

SITUATION: Your man consummates the relationship by giving all of himself to you. He confides that he trusts and wants you to be the woman in his life. He wants to meet your family and for you to meet his.

THOUGHT: Wow! I really like this guy-he's doing things the right way. Girl, you better go 'head with your bad self. You must be putting it down right! The question that millions of women want to know is: Does a man know if you are the one for him the first time he meets you? Well, ladies hold on to your seats. That answer will be revealed in a later chapter. I do believe that a man knows when you are the one for him. He ponders and analyzes how you'll fit into his life and if he'll be able to satisfy or provide for you. Then, he gives you the green light to be in a full-bloom, committed relationship with him. He wants to see you regularly. He wants you to leave your clothes in his closet like they're a permanent fixture in the house. There are introductions to family and friends; the parades and functions around town; the two of you are officially an item. Doesn't it feel good when a man welcomes you into his life and you welcome him into yours? He's your man and you're his woman. Nothing beats the way you feel. New love is such an explosion of goodness! Love is the greatest gift to mankind.

How Would You Handle It?

_____

_____

_____

_____

What Does God's Word Say About It?

If I speak with the tongues of men and of angels, but have not love, I am become sounding brass, or a clanging cymbal. And if I have the gift of prophecy, and know all mysteries and all knowledge; and if I have all faith, so as to remove mountains, but have not love, I am nothing. And if I bestow all my goods to feed the poor, and if I give my body to be burned, but have not love, it profiteth me nothing.
I CORINTHIANS 13:1-3

v. 4-7 *Love suffereth long, and is kind; love envieth not; love vaunteth not itself, is not puffed up, doth not behave itself unseemly, seeketh not its own, is not provoked, taketh not account of evil; rejoiceth not in unrighteousness, but rejoiceth with the truth; beareth all things, believeth all things, hopeth all things, endureth all things*

v. 13 *But now abideth faith, hope, love, these three; and the greatest of these is love.*

SITUATION: You're single in the ministry and trying to practice abstinence, but your partner insists that you continue having sex with him since you guys are going to be getting married. Prior to accepting your calling, you were having sex for about 18 years, although you were both saved. Because of your spiritual conviction, you decide that you no longer want to have sex. However, you feel that your partner is a true man of God; a man after God's own heart.

However, he has a thorn in his side, and that's a sexual appetite for his longtime partner.

THOUGHT: The key statement here is, "going to be getting married," which means you are not married at the present time. You need to make it clear to him that you do not want to continue fornicating and that you are serious about your walk with God. If he doesn't understand or like it, he can follow the "exit" sign out of your life. When you take your relationship with God serious, you have a new way of thinking. It's important for others to know how important your beliefs are to you. Check yourself to make sure you haven't become complacent by continuing to do the things you were doing before you were converted. When you decide to change your lifestyle, it needs to be a 360-degree turn-if not, you confuse others and they begin to question your walk. They may not take your Christianity seriously. You need to address this issue head-on, so your man will understand that you're not playing. Anything less than that will make you feel like you're being taken advantage of. If your partner really loves you and understands that you are committed to your relationship with God, he'll change his behavior as well, or move on. It's sad to say, but it happens like that sometimes. Marriage gives him the rights to the privilege of sex, not longevity.

How Would You Handle It?

_____

_____

_____

_____

What Does God's Word Say About It?

Therefore let us also, seeing we are compassed about with so great a cloud of witnesses, lay aside every weight, and the sin which doth so easily beset us, and let us run with patience the race that is set before us, HEBREWS 12:1

Be subject therefore unto God; but resist the devil, and he will flee from you. JAMES 4:7

Or know ye not that the unrighteous shall not inherit the kingdom of God? Be not deceived: neither fornicators, nor idolaters, nor adulterers, nor effeminate, nor abusers of themselves with men, nor thieves, nor covetous, nor drunkards, nor revilers, nor extortioners, shall inherit the kingdom of God. I CORINTHIANS 6:9-10

SITUATION: Your significant other is currently going through a difficult time in his life and hasn't had the desire to be intimate with you. He explains that he's still attracted to and turned on by you, but because of the mental strain, just can't focus at the moment. You advise him that you're okay with the fact that the two of you are not being intimate and convince him that you're there to support him in whatever he's going through.

THOUGHT: It sounds as if you have an adult relationship going on-I mean, where grown folks communicate and support one another for real.

How amazing, because an immature person wouldn't have been able to handle the fact that their partner wasn't having sex with them. It also sounds like the two of you have a lot of respect for one another. We put too much stock into sex these days. While it is an important part of a relationship, it's not the glue that holds the relationship together. Furthermore, you would probably want to have your spouse be present in mind, body and soul instead of just going through the motions. To a man, sex is just sex, but add love and emotions and it means much more. "Real love, I'm searching for the real love, someone to set my heart free, real love, I'm searching for a real love." Now, that's the way Mary J. breaks it down. At the end of the day, aren't we all looking for something real and tangible?

How Would You Handle It?

_____

_____

_____

_____

What Does God's Word Say About It?

> _For God so loved the world, that he gave his only begotten Son, that whosoever believeth on him should not perish, but have eternal life._
> JOHN 3:16

> _Love suffereth long, and is kind; love envieth not; love vaunteth not itself, is not puffed up._ I CORINTHIANS 13:4

INSECURITIES

SITUATION: You're dating a brotha who is very jealous. He lives in another city, but called to see if you were home one evening and when you weren't, he began to question your children about where you were. He then drove 180 miles (in another female's car) to see if you had someone at your house.

THOUGHT: Now, I would say that's Inspector Gadget at your service. Two things I learned at an early age is that: a jealous man won't do and a young fool is just as bad as an old fool. This is a dangerous person-like a time bomb getting ready to explode. You should quickly try and defuse the problem by letting this man know that you're not cheating on him. The likely case is that he is cheating, so he thinks that you are, too. It's the oldest trick in the book. Men really know how to reverse that thing don't they? It would also be a good thing to ask him not to question the children. If they say you're not home, then he should leave a message for you to call him back. He should leave the kids out of it, because kids will tell the truth and nothing but the truth, so help them God! Now, if this man drives over 180 miles to see that you are, or are not cheating, there's a bigger problem at hand that you need to deal with. You need to get out of that relationship fast, unless you have given him reason to suspect otherwise. The fact that he went to great lengths to drive that distance (and in another female's car), says that he's very jealous or expects something from you. Don't sleep on this type of behavior. On the other hand, the question should have been: Who's the female that allowed him to travel that distance in her car to see if you were cheating on him?

How Would You Handle It?

_____

_____

_____

_____

What Does God's Word Say About It?

> *But if ye have bitter jealousy and faction in your heart, glory not and lie not against the truth. This wisdom is not a wisdom that cometh down from above, but is earthly, sensual, devilish. For where jealousy and faction are, there is confusion and every vile deed.*
> JAMES 3:14-16

> *Let us walk becomingly, as in the day; not in revelling and drunkenness, not in chambering and wantonness, not in strife and jealousy.* ROMANS 13:13

SITUATION: You have been married for the past three and a half years. Your spouse buys you everything you could ever want or imagine. However, after relocating to his area, with a whole new life and job after marriage, you discover that he's very jealous and insecure. It's beginning to destroy your relationship and marriage. It's so bad that when you go to visit your girlfriend, who lives in a secluded area off the highway, he shows up, rings the doorbell and casually tells you that he was in the area. Then, when you visit your family, he calls to make sure you are there. On another occasion, when you go visit your good friend during a special time in her life, your husband complains about how you are never home due to your new job and travel, instead of wishing your friend well. He also confronts your boss about your travel. Then he has the nerve to tell you that he didn't sign up for "all of that."

THOUGHT: I'm sure that was the straw that broke the camel's back. I know after all of that you were ready to scream! You were enraged to the point of no return and I'm sure you didn't sign up for all of that either. This brother needs some serious counseling and I mean with the quickness, before he does something he'll regret. This is a serious problem that needs to be addressed immediately. You need to find a way to express the severity of the situation to him; it could cost your marriage if he doesn't do something about his behavior and soon. Now, I have to also address your safety. If your husband takes deranged actions, he could also cause harm to you. You need to be very careful. Pay special attention to his actions, and make provision to get to a safe place, if necessary. It would also be a good idea to let family and friends know your whereabouts at all times, especially when you're traveling. Be vigilant, as you don't know what he's capable of, and you don't want to add fuel to the fire.

How Would You Handle It?

_____

_____

_____

_____

What Does God's Word Say About It?

> For jealousy is the rage of a man; And he will not spare in the day of vengeance. PROVERBS 6:34

> Wrath is cruel, and anger is overwhelming; But who is able to stand before jealousy? PROVERBS 27:4

> Now the works of the flesh are manifest, which are these: fornication, uncleanness, lasciviousness, idolatry, sorcery, enmities, strife, jealousies, wraths, factions, divisions, parties, envyings, drunkenness, revellings, and such like; of which I forewarn you, even as I did forewarn you, that they who practise such things shall not inherit the kingdom of God. GALATIANS 5:19-21

—⚮—

SITUATION: You have a girlfriend and every time she gets a new significant other she stops communicating with you. If she doesn't stop communicating completely, she only calls when her significant other isn't around.

THOUGHT: This sounds like an insecure sister to me. What a selfish thing to do, especially if the two of you are really good friends. Why wouldn't you want to share your newfound love and happiness with those who are apart of your life? She needs to learn how to date without losing herself in her significant other. There's no need to isolate herself from family and friends. If she doesn't stop this behavior, she might end up losing a good friend, altogether. It's always a good thing to get to know a guy and make sure he's going to be around for a minute, before introducing him to your family and friends. However, it's never a good idea to cut yourself off from the ones who love and care for you. Relationships are complicated, but people don't have to be.

How Would You Handle It?

_____

_____

_____

_____

What Does God's Word Say About It?

He that maketh many friends doeth it to his own destruction; But there is a friend that sticketh closer than a brother. PROVERBS 18:24

SITUATION: You've been in a relationship with a man for six years. He's given you no indication that he's cheating. He's a deacon at his church and does right by you in every way. Yet, you insist on snooping around by tapping into his emails and voice mails to see if he's communicating with other women. However, you have a longtime friend who's a bodybuilder. He sends you pictures of himself in Speedos and of him working out. This friend also came to spend Christmas with you and your family while your man was spending the holidays with his daughter. How do you think your man would respond if he knew this behavior was going on?

THOUGHT: It always looks different when the shoe is on the other foot. It appears you have a trust issue and it doesn't lie within your man, because he's been true and hasn't given you reason to believe otherwise. There's an old saying, "If you go looking for something you just might find what you're looking for." You should stop this behavior unless he gives you a reason to seek after something. Furthermore, it's also wise to stop entertaining your male friend who continues to send you pictures of his body. They are undoubtedly sexy and might become a temptation to you in the long run. There's just something about a brotha in Speedos, especially if he's a handsome brotha, and that body's tight and right! You might be tempted to call or visit him, which could lead to something more. It's not good to play with fire-you might get burned. Evaluate your reasons for checking up on your man, as well as your motives behind your relationship with your male friend.

How Would You Handle It?

_____

_____

_____

_____

What Does God's Word Say About It?

> *Watch and pray, that ye enter not into temptation: the spirit indeed is willing, but the flesh is weak.* MATTHEW 26:41

—⚹—

SITUATION: What should you do when a man tells you over and over that he loves you, but always accuses you of cheating on him? He pops up at your job while talking to you on the cell phone, brings flowers home, but still accuses you of cheating. Then, he chooses to not be intimate with you at times, stating that he doesn't want sex to be boring.

THOUGHT: Boring, for whom? I would think that the two of you would be in control of that. Several things come to mind after reading this sitchiation : the brotha himself is cheating, he's insecure and jealous, or has been cheated on so badly that he's scarred for life and just can't trust a sistah anymore, even if he wanted to. If the last reason I mentioned is the case, you're going to have to do a lot to gain his trust. That would take much prayer, and there's still a possibility it might not work, depending on the depth of his scars. Sometimes, when brothas come bearing gifts, it's a sign of guilt. The fact that he doesn't want to have sex is probably because he's already had it somewhere else. I'm not male-bashing here at all-just speaking from prior experience. If your man has had sex elsewhere, then in the words of Bette Davis, "Fasten your seat belts, it's going to be a bumpy night."

How Would You Handle It?

What Does God's Word Say About It?

> *But like as he who called you is holy, be ye yourselves also holy in all manner of living.* 1 PETER 1:15

—※—

SITUATION: You have been dating a man for almost seven years. There hasn't been any discussion concerning marriage. You recently agreed to see other people. You join an online dating site and meet an eligible bachelor who is educated, professional, and financially set. However, he's only average height, which is sort of a problem for you, but you continue to speak to him. You soon meet and start spending time with one another. This man begins showering you with gifts and money and expresses that he would also like to give you a credit card so that you'll be able to get whatever you need. You're very impressed and love the attention. As it turns out, this man's height is also a problem for him. He expresses that he's surprised that you even wanted to be with him. He also confides that his height is the reason he felt he wasn't able to get a date in such a long time. In the midst of all the excitement, your ex calls and proposes to you over the phone, saying that he is finally ready to marry you. Now you're confused, because you like the attention you've been getting from your new friend, but you still have a problem with his height. Your ex, on the other hand, is much taller. Huh?

THOUGHT: Sometimes great things come in small packages, but if that's not your cup of tea, then you shouldn't entertain it. It seems like you need to come to terms with what's most important to you in a relationship. The fact that the new guy is showering you with gifts and money seems to be clouding your judgment. The other issue at hand is why it has taken your male friend of seven years, so long to decide that he finally wants to marry you. Sounds fishy to me. Did he just realize after all this time that you are the "one"? Now, let me address the new brother-doesn't he know that money can't buy you love? No amount of money or gift giving can truly make a person happy. You really have to be happy and satisfied with who you are before you can please or be pleased by someone else. Although money can make you comfortable and happy, if that's the main reason you're with him, what happens when it's no longer there? Joy-which surpasses happiness-comes from God Almighty. He's the only one who can give you what you truly need, in addition to the desires of your heart. Instead of looking to a man to fill the void in your heart, try looking to God as your source of joy and fulfillment.

How Would You Handle It?

_____

_____

_____

_____

What Does God's Word Say About It?

>*Delight thyself also in Jehovah; And he will give thee the desires of thy heart.* PSALM: 37:4

—⚭—

MARRIED MAN
"Secret Lover"

SITUATION: You just finished making love to a married man and he says, "Wow! This changes things." Then he goes on to say that he doesn't want anyone to get hurt.

THOUGHT: First of all, you probably shouldn't be in this situation in the first place, but let's keep it real; in life these things do occur. However, it doesn't make it right. The fact that you had sex with this man doesn't change things because he's still and will probably continue to be married, whether you choose to continue to see him or not. You should explain that you will not be calling or riding by his house, nor should he come to your place, unannounced. It's called, "R-E-S-P-E-C-T, find out what it means to me!" You should send that man back home to his wife quick, fast and in a hurry, without a second thought. Then ask God for forgiveness of that sin and pray that you don't find yourself in that state of weakness ever again.

How Would You Handle It?

_____

_____

_____

_____

What Does God's Word Say About It?

Wives, be in subjection unto your own husbands, as unto the Lord.
EPHESIANS 5:22

Husbands, love your wives, even as Christ also loved the church, and gave himself up for it. EPHESIANS 5:25

Now concerning the things whereof ye wrote: It is good for a man not to touch a woman. But, because of fornications, let each man have his own wife, and let each woman have her own husband. Let the husband render unto the wife her due: and likewise also the wife unto the husband. I CORINTHIANS 7:1-3

SITUATION: You have an extramarital affair with an old flame. Do you tell your spouse or not?

THOUGHT: There are differences of opinion on this type of situation. One might say to be honest and up-front by confessing your adulterous behavior, while another might say, "I'll never tell-I'll take it to the grave." Honesty is always the best policy.

How Would You Handle It?

_____

_____

_____

_____

What Does God's Word Say About It?

That by two immutable things, in which it is impossible for God to lie, we may have a strong encouragement, who have fled for refuge to lay hold of the hope set before us. HEBREWS 6:18

He that is faithful in a very little is faithful also in much: and he that is unrighteous in a very little is unrighteous also in much. LUKE 16:10

The thoughts of the righteous are just; But the counsels of the wicked are deceit. PROVERBS 12:5

—⚊—

SITUATION: You are a single woman, dating a married man whose wife works with you. You both get pregnant by him around the same time. You insist on playing games with this woman. Because you have a key to this man's truck, you go out on your lunch break and move the vehicle from one side of the building to the other. When you go to this man's house (that he shares with his wife), you take personal things that belong to her or move things around to let her know you've been there. You get angry because her sisters don't care for you or invite you to any of their functions, while other co-workers are invited. On top of all this, you attend the same church as this woman and her sisters.

THOUGHT: Ok, you need to get your own man! Leave that married man alone. Are you so desperate for a man that you have to hang on to one that belongs to someone else? I don't care what problems exist between them-someone else's husband will never be your husband. Furthermore, you'll never succeed by behaving so foolishly. As far as the sisters go, you better thank God that they didn't catch you alone and beat your butt real good. My, how times have changed! Can you say death sentence?

How Would You Handle It?

_____

_____

_____

_____

What Does God's Word Say About It?

Let marriage be had in honor among all, and let the bed be undefiled: for fornicators and adulterers God will judge. HEBREWS 13:4

SITUATION: You meet this guy who falls madly in love with you at first sight. This brotha is 6'4 and fine from head to toe. First, you are on a casual basis with one another, speaking only when you see one another. Then, after your male friend makes you mad, you agree to meet this guy for drinks. He's a perfect gentleman: great conversation, he pays for the meal, walks you to your car and plants a kiss on you that lights up the sky. It's déjà vu and brings back memories of something you once liked, but knew wasn't good for you. As time goes on, you begin talking to this man every day, for long periods of time. He begins to come over to your place after work and stays until the wee hours of the morning, but nothing sexual occurs. After several months, he expresses that he's interested in making your relationship official, so the two of you proceed accordingly. Everything is going well, when your brother informs you that this man is married! You are conflicted because you can see the love this man has for you in his eyes and through his expressions. A year goes by and the two of you enter into a business partnership together. Because of the partnership, you feel it would be best for the two of you to stop seeing one another. His wife confronts you and says, "You need to learn how to handle your man."

THOUGHT: Cricket, Cricket, Cricket! His wife told you to learn how to handle your man? From the words of Malcolm X, "Oh, I say and I say it again, ya been had! Ya been took! Ya been hoodwinked! Bamboozled! Led astray! Run amok! This is what He does." It sounds like this sister knew all along what had been going on between the two of you, or she must have seen the look in his eyes when you were around. You need to get out of that mess quickly. I'll say it again, someone else's husband will never be yours.

How Would You Handle It?

_____

_____

_____

_____

What Does God's Word Say About It?

Flee fornication. Every sin that a man doeth is without the body; but he that committeth fornication sinneth against his own body. I CORINTHIANS 6:18

But, because of fornications, let each man have his own wife, and let each woman have her own husband. I CORINTHIANS 7:2

———————————————— —ɷ— ————————————————

SITUATION: What if you were asked to be the third wife in a Muslim relationship and told that you could pick any place to live and the luxury car of your choice?

THOUGHT: This is pure craziness! Why would a man need multiple wives? Does he love them all the same, or does he use them for different functions? Resist the temptation to engage in this type of relationship. You can be in a healthy relationship with a man who will love and want to be with you and only you. Don't lower your standards, and knowingly continue to be in a relationship with someone else's husband. God's word teaches that one man and one woman leave and cleave to become one.

How Would You Handle It?

——————————————————————————————

——————————————————————————————

——————————————————————————————

——————————————————————————————

What Does God's Word Say About It?

*In like manner, ye wives, be in subjection to your won husbands;
that, even if any obey not the word, they may without the word
be gained by the behavior of their wives; beholding your chaste
behavior coupled with fear. Whose adorning let it not be the
outward adorning of braiding the hair, and of wearing jewels of
gold, or of putting on apparel; but let it be the hidden man of the
heart, in the incorruptible apparel of a meek and quiet spirit, which
is in the sight of God of great price. For after this manner aforetime
the holy women also, who hoped in God, adorned themselves, being
in subjection to their own husbands: as Sarah obeyed Abraham,
calling him lord: whose children ye now are, if ye do well, and are
not put in fear by any terror.* I PETER 3:1-6*

*The bishop therefore must be without reproach, the husband of one
wife, temperate, sober-minded, orderly, given to hospitality, apt to
teach;* I TIMOTHY 3:2

SITUATION: An ex male friend that you haven't talked to in over a
decade inboxes you on Facebook, stating that he ran across a letter that
you wrote him in 2003 and was reminiscing on how much fun you both
had when you were dating, and how he used to drive long distance
to see you. He is now married with four children and proceeds to tell
you that he is moving driving distance away from you...

THOUGHT: Are you kidding me, did he just throw that out to see if you were going to bite? Does he actually think that you're seeking a secret lover here? The man is married with children-excuse me, four children. The last time you were together was 11 years ago. Does he think you're just going to give him your address and resume the relationship? You shouldn't waste time by responding to his message. I know the ratio of men to women is slim, but resorting to seeing someone else's husband is not a smart option. There are still good men out there. Don't settle for someone who is seeking an affair, after reconnecting with you via social media.

How Would You Handle It?

_____

_____

_____

_____

What Does God's Word Say About It?

> *But I say unto you, that every one that looketh on a woman to lust after her hath committed adultery with her already in his heart.*
> MATTHEW 5:28

> *For freedom did Christ set us free: stand fast therefore, and be not entangled again in a yoke of bondage.* GALATIANS 5:1

PLAYA, PLAYER, PLAY ON

SITUATION: Would you agree to date a man who's been inconsistent in the past? He schedules dates with you but has only been present for one date since you started seeing him. It's just excuse after excuse. He promised to attend your birthday celebration, but was a no-show. You recall your first conversation over the phone, in which he informed you that he doesn't "chase women." You calmly replied stating, "I don't chase men either, so I guess we won't be chasing one another."

THOUGHT: I guess he was letting you know in the beginning what things would be like. This relationship wouldn't work if his past proved to be so inconsistent. He should actually be present in order to be in a relationship. Daily interaction isn't a must (if that's what you agree to), but you both should be prepared to be active participants in the relationship. No true love connection can exist unless you both agree. After all, who wants half a man or half a woman? It should be all or nothing. It sounds like this player was either married or involved with someone else and just wanted to see which one he was going to get his hooks into first. In the end, it's just not worth it.

How Would You Handle It?

_____

_____

_____

_____

What Does God's Word Say About It?

Again I say unto you, that if two of you shall agree on earth as touching anything that they shall ask, it shall be done for them of my Father who is in heaven. For where two or three are gathered together in my name, there am I in the midst of them. MATTHEW 18:19-20

SITUATION: You're dating an ex-military guy, shortly after he gets out of the service. He moves in with you and you begin dating. As it turns out, he's very jealous. He denies it, but his actions show otherwise. Whenever you ask him to go out with you, he doesn't go, but shortly after you reach your destination, he shows up. You end the relationship. This guy actually moves in with your father while looking for work, and has all kinds of women calling there and leaving messages for him. However, he says he wants to get back together with you.

THOUGHT: It sounds like this guy is a jealous womanizer. Get him out of your life immediately! He's not ready for a commitment and clearly wants to continue on in his womanizing ways. News alert: Run, Forest! Run!

How Would You Handle It?

_____

_____

_____

_____

What Does God's Word Say About It?

But if they have not continency, let them marry: for it is better to marry than to burn. 1 CORINTHIANS 7:9

Abstain from every form of evil. I THESSALONIANS 5:22

———————————— —m— ————————————

SITUATION: While dating a "baller" who owns a game room/pool hall, you come in one night to see him, after class. You find him sitting at the bar, entertaining some woman and her girlfriends. He immediately starts an argument with you, to throw you off and get you to leave. He accuses you of having an affair with his uncle and disrespects you by calling you out of your name.

THOUGHT: Well, this is clearly reverse psychology. It's his way of distracting you so you don't confront him about the other woman. Move on, knowing there's someone out there who wants to be with you, and will treat you right and not call you names. As children, we used to say, "Sticks and stones may break my bones, but words will never hurt me." Well, words actually do hurt and keep us from moving forward. We have to learn to move on past the pain, believing God for deliverance from those who have hurt us, by pressing into His presence. He is able to heal your brokenness and to put you back together again.

How Would You Handle It?

_____

_____

_____

_____

What Does God's Word Say About It?

> *Oil and perfume rejoice the heart; So doth the sweetness of a man's friend that cometh of hearty counsel.* PROVERBS 27:9

> *How fair is thy love, my sister, my bride! How much better is thy love than wine! And the fragrance of thine oils than all manner of spices! Thy lips, O my bride, drop as the honeycomb: Honey and milk are under thy tongue; And the smell of thy garments is like the smell of Lebanon.* SONG OF SOLOMON 4:10-11

> *Be not unequally yoked with unbelievers: for what fellowship have righteousness and iniquity? or what communion hath light with darkness? And what concord hath Christ with Belial? or what portion hath a believer with an unbeliever?* II CORINTHIANS 6:14-15

———————————————— —₪— ————————————————

SITUATION: You meet a brother at a social event who's an upcoming comedian. The two of you hit it off pretty well. You exchange numbers, hang out following the event, and continue to see one another as time permits. Later, he starts working for a company that you were formerly employed at as a sales manager. While in town on business, he invites you to his hotel room for drinks. Due to some car trouble, you arrive a little late. As you are looking for his room, you see another young lady who appears to be looking for the same room. You finally find his room and knock on the door. He informs you that you're late and he already has someone else coming, and slams the door in your face. You are shocked and shame-faced all at the same time. How could he do this to you?

THOUGHT: Now, this is deception at its finest. Obviously, this brother has done this before. It sounds like it's his mode of operation. He's a playa and you have just been played. This happens to us all, at one time or another. Chalk it up as experience and learn not to be so gullible next time. Sometimes, all a man wants is the "cookie"-once he gets it, he no longer has need of you. It looks like he was not only playing you, but another gullible sister in the process. Better luck next time. This kind of behavior needs to be called out when it occurs. Talk about a real snake in the grass!

How Would You Handle It?

_____

_____

_____

_____

What Does God's Word Say About It?

And Jesus answered and said unto them, Take heed that no man lead
you astray. MATTHEW 24:4

And have no fellowship with the unfruitful works of darkness, but
rather even reprove them. EPHESIANS 5:11

———————————— —₥— ————————————

SITUATION: A man has a "love jones" for a woman who lives out
of state, but he is unsure if he will be able to maintain a long-distance
relationship. This woman was initially interested in the man, but as time
went on, she developed an interest in another man (a married man!) who
lived in her area. She eventually cast the first man aside. This man has
not come to terms with the fact that the woman is no longer interested in
him and continues to vie for her attention, to no avail. The woman has
blatantly disrespected him, yet has asked him to provide the bankroll
for her recent business venture and he is actually considering the offer.
When should a person realize that they are being taken advantage of and
a relationship is not conducive to their well-being?

THOUGIIT: It sounds like this sister has a little "Use-A-Brother" in her
system. She is seeking a financier that will set her up on Easy Street. If
brothers continue to fall for her game, then it serves them right to be
taken by a "femme fatale." Sisters like this make it hard for women who
are truly willing to put their time in for a good man. On the other hand,

the brother in this scenario, needs to stop falling for her tricks. The red flags are always there-it just depends on whether or not we want to see them. Sometimes, the player gets played. "Don't hate the player, hate the game."

How Would You Handle It?

_____

_____

_____

_____

What Does God's Word Say About It?

> _And the serpent said unto the woman, Ye shall not surely die:_
> GENESIS 3:4

> _And be not fashioned according to this world: but be ye transformed by the renewing of your mind, and ye may prove what is the good and acceptable and perfect will of God._ ROMANS 12:2

—⟋⟍—

SITUATION: I have a girlfriend who's really living it up, I mean playing guys like they're "The Price Is Right" game show and she's the winner of all three doors! Check this out: She's dating three different guys at the same time. One is a handsome man from another country, who wants to take her to New York. The next man is giving her a car and taking her on a weekend getaway, and the third man is taking her to Las Vegas. She feels as if she's living in a dream world and to top it all off, two of these men know about one another and are trying to out-do each other. My friend feels her life is exciting and that she won't have this type of fun when she gets older. She's taking advantage of it now, while it lasts. Oy vey!

THOUGHT: It is so unfair for my friend to be dating these guys at the same time. She's making it hard for women who could be truly committed to an exclusive relationship with them. Do these guys really know about one another? If so, why are they accepting this behavior? Someone always gets hurt in these types of situations. When you play with fire, you get burned. The Word of God cautions us about serving two masters (Matt 6:24). My friend needs to understand that these brothers are giving her gifts and taking her on trips, while keeping her in a sinful state of living. What a high cost to pay, when God's plan has no charge.

How Would You Handle It?

_____

_____

_____

_____

What Does God's Word Say About It?

> *No man can serve two masters; for either he will hate the one, and love the other; or else he will hold to one, and despise the other. Ye cannot serve God and mammon* MATTHEW 6:24

UNPROTECTED SEX

"Wrap It Up"

SITUATION: You have unprotected sex with someone who is HIV-positive, several times. Would you say this is a prescription written for death?

THOUGHT: Why would you continue to have unprotected sex with this person given the risk? The blessing in the midst of this behavior would be if you never contracted the virus. The best practice is to always "wrap it up." Even better than that, how about practicing abstinence until you get married? Just because someone looks healthy doesn't mean they're not infected. Looks can be deceiving. No matter how you feel about the person, you still have to protect yourself.

How Would You Handle It?

_____

_____

_____

What Does God's Word Say About It?

> *Jehovah is on my side; I will not fear: What can man do unto me?*
> PSALM 118:6

He that dwelleth in the secret place of the Most High Shall abide under the shadow of the Almighty. I will say of Jehovah, He is my refuge and my fortress; My God, in whom I trust. For he will deliver thee from the snare of the fowler, And from the deadly pestilence. He will cover thee with his pinions, And under his wings shalt thou take refuge: His truth is a shield and a buckler. Thou shalt not be afraid for the terror by night, Nor for the arrow that flieth by day; For the pestilence that walketh in darkness, Nor for the destruction that wasteth at noonday. A thousand shall fall at thy side, And ten thousand at thy right hand; But it shall not come nigh thee.

PSALM 91:1-7

—⟋⟍—

SITUATION: You're in a relationship with a guy and his ex-girlfriend informs you that she stopped dating him because he gave her an STD. This was her way of letting you know that he was seeing the both of you at the same time. Do you take her word for it and confront the brother, or do you go to your doctor and have a checkup to confirm the information to be true?

THOUGHT: It's always a good idea to have your facts. You should definitely go to the doctor for a check-up and any necessary treatment. Then you should let that brother have it! Now, you have to accept some responsibility for your carelessness as well, because you were having unprotected sex with him. We want to feel as though the person we're sleeping with is not sleeping with someone else. In reality, it's never a good thing to assume, when we can do it right the first time by wrapping it up. It's embarrassing to both parties when an unexpected "surprise" shows up. Trust goes right out the window, not to mention you're stuck with a disease you need treatment for or even something that you might not be able to get rid of for the rest of your life! Let that trifling brother go on about his business and take that STD with him.

How Would You Handle It?

_____

_____

_____

_____

What Does God's Word Say About It?

And he said, If thou wilt diligently hearken to the voice of Jehovah thy God, and wilt do that which is right in his eyes, and wilt give ear to his commandments, and keep all his statutes, I will put none of the diseases upon thee, which I have put upon the Egyptians: for I am Jehovah that healeth thee. EXODUS 15:26

Bless Jehovah, O my soul, And forget not all his benefits: Who forgiveth all thine iniquities; Who healeth all thy diseases; Who redeemeth thy life from destruction; Who crowneth thee with lovingkindness and tender mercies. PSALM 103:2-4

SITUATION: I have a girlfriend who's just foolishly in love with men. She called me on one occasion, all excited to tell me that a particular man-the one that every woman wants to be with-asked her to spend the weekend with him at his elegant mansion in the hills. She said his bedroom had a great view, overlooking the lake. A room with a real view! This brother was divorced because he cheated on his wife and brought home a STD that she's unable to get rid of. It broke up his happy home and left his children without their father. My friend was fully aware of the situation, so I asked if she planned on picking up some condoms. She simply said, "No." I rest my case with this dumb bunny!

THOUGHT: The Word says that the truth we know sets us free , and I've also heard that we do better when we know better." Well, I would like to add my own version: "The truth that we know should set us free, but we have to want to be free." The consequences of sin truly effects all involved. In my girlfriend's case, she knew right from wrong and knew that this man was a carrier of a particular STD and had infected others. Why would she still want to hang out with him and have unprotected sex? It doesn't make sense to risk your life for a good time. There's nothing in the world that good. You are writing your own death sentence when you behave in such a manner and it serves you right because you're selfish and want to do what you want to, with whomever you choose. You have to take full responsibility for whatever happens. Now, as for this man, he needs to be open about being a carrier of a disease and practice safe sex. Nothing bothers me more than to have someone take my choices away from me. I'd much rather have you tell me what type of tea is in my china and let me decide if I want to drink it or not.

How Would You Handle It?

_____

_____

_____

_____

What Does God's Word Say About It?

But be ye doers of the word, and not hearers only, deluding your own selves. For if any one is a hearer of the word and not a doer, he is like unto a man beholding his natural face in a mirror: for he beholdeth himself, and goeth away, and straightway forgetteth what manner of man he was. But he that looketh into the perfect law, the law of liberty, and so continueth, being not a hearer that forgetteth but a doer that worketh, this man shall be blessed in his doing. If any man thinketh himself to be religious, while he bridleth not his tongue but deceiveth his heart, this man's religion is vain. Pure religion and undefiled before our God and Father is this, to visit the fatherless and widows in their affliction, and to keep oneself unspotted from the world. JAMES 1:22-27

Part III

"Are You Kidding Me?"

Don't be Stuck on Stupid all Your Natural-born Life. . .

Are You CraZy or Just Hard -up for a Man?

CraZy-N-Love

SITUATION: Have you ever loved a man so much that it makes you cry, and you knew he meant you no good? You would melt at the sight and touch of this man but every time you put your hope and trust in him, his unfaithfulness and disloyalty were revealed. You would cry your heart out and forgive him, only to find out that he would do it to you over and over again. The last straw was when you discovered that the person he was messing around with was your very own best friend; the one you confided in; the one who knew all your secrets; and the one who knew exactly what to do to get your man.

THOUGHT: The same thing that makes you laugh is the same thing that makes you cry. It's not a good idea to share all your secrets with your girlfriends, especially when it comes to your man. Sometimes, they can use that same information to lure your man right into their arms, their beds and anything else they want or need. You talking about low-down and dirty-I assure you, it does happen. It's okay to talk about surface stuff with your friends, but the intriguing parts of your relationship between you and your man should only be shared between the two of you. Be wary of girlfriends who want to skip the chitchat and get down to the real nitty-gritty details about your relationship.

How Would You Handle It?

_____

_____

What Does God's Word Say About It?

Avenge not yourselves, beloved, but give place unto the wrath of God: for it is written, Vengeance belongeth unto me; I will recompense, saith the Lord. ROMANS 12:19

For he is a minister of God to thee for good. But if thou do that which is evil, be afraid; for he beareth not the sword in vain: for he is a minister of God, an avenger for wrath to him that doeth evil. ROMANS 13:4

———————————— —ᴟ— ————————————

SITUATION: You have a "thing" for a brother, but he won't give you the time of day. You call and leave messages for him to call you back. He usually doesn't but when he does, he acts very nonchalant. He does, however, find the time to send you text messages like, "You're a good woman; thanks for your support; call when you can; I need to hear your voice; you're special to me; I have so much love and respect for you; I'm glad you're in my life." When you finally get him on the phone, he acts distant or says something to get you off the phone and doesn't call back. He promises to come see you or take you out, but never follows through.

THOUGHT: Dang, I'm bored already with this dude. It seems like he's impressed only with himself and what someone else does to pump him up and support him. Either he doesn't know how to give it back in return, he's just a boring person, or he's playing games with you my sistah. On the other hand, he's probably a very good-looking guy and is accustomed to the ladies just falling all over him. If that's the case, throw your hand back in and ask to be dealt another one that doesn't include the likes of that type of behavior. Who has time to spend it on someone who doesn't appreciate the love, support, or encouragement that you're giving? You need to tell that brotha you don't have any time for games. Send that brotha packing the same way he came. Why is it that we always want the ones that don't want us? Actions speak louder than words. Don't make someone have to tell you twice. Even a dog has sense enough to move on if it's mistreated. Recognize what's happening right before your very own eyes.

How Would You Handle It?

_____

_____

_____

_____

What Does God's Word Say About It?

> *There can be neither Jew nor Greek, there can be neither bond nor free, there can be no male and female; for ye all are one man in Christ Jesus.* GALATIANS 3:28

*For we must all be made manifest before the judgment-seat of Christ;
that each one may receive the things done in the body, according to
what he hath done, whether it be good or bad.* II CORINTHIANS 5:10

SITUATION: You've been dating this man for over 18 years and have experienced everything under the sun with him: cheating (a lot of it); baby mama drama; physical, mental, and emotional abuse. Your battle scars are evident. You've experienced so much heartache and pain that it's hard for you to trust anyone else. There has been lie after lie. You need the truth, the whole truth, and nothing but the truth, so help you God. You were even exposed to drugs because of your relationship with this man and you wonder why he never married you, although he kept saying he would. You loved this man and wanted nobody else except him.

THOUGHT: You're kidding me right? All the stuff this man put you through and you still wanted to be his wife? I guess love does conquer all. At this point in your life, if it's not working, don't force it. If he's abusing you, lying to you, and giving you baby mama drama, I would encourage you to move on and find someone who will give more of what you need and less negativity. None of us are perfect. However, there are still some really good men out there who come with a little less baggage. Do you really want to continue living your life like this? I wouldn't wish this life on my worst enemy. We hold on to stuff that God Himself wants to deliver us from, but can't because we won't let Him. If you let go of this bad relationship, you might be able to get what God really has in store for you. In many cases, it's already there, waiting for you to surrender.

How Would You Handle It?

What Does God's Word Say About It?

> *Now unto him that is able to do exceeding abundantly above all that we ask or think, according to the power that worketh in us, unto him be the glory in the church and in Christ Jesus unto all generations for ever and ever. Amen.* EPHESIANS 3:20-21

SITUATION: Why is it that when you're in a new relationship, your mind is all over the place, like a crazy person? Is he going to call me; did I say the right thing when we talked last; should I call or text him; will he think I'm desperate; does he really like me; am I sexy enough; do I satisfy him; is he seeing or talking to someone else when I'm not around? By the end of the day, you're a nervous wreck.

THOUGHT: Wow-just reading that made me tired! I advise you to take a "chill pill" and calm your nerves. When you realize that you're not in control of anything, it makes the journey much better and much easier to handle. You cannot control what another person does or how they think. If they have it in their mind to do something, you can't change or stop it. People are who they are. If the person is trustworthy, then that's what they'll present. If their low-down and dirty, then that's what you'll get. I would advise that you don't get involved with those who are accustomed to cheating on you; those who feel that they have to be dating you and 20 other women at the same time. The world is filled with all types of women, but that doesn't mean they have to date every woman they meet. Some men have a woman to satisfy every need they have. If you find yourself dating this type of man, then you really don't have anything to begin with. Let him go just as fast as he came into your life. If you can't trust him, then you don't need him. Nuff said!

How Would You Handle It?

_____

_____

_____

_____

What Does God's Word Say About It?

> *Therefore I say unto you, be not anxious for your life, what ye shall eat, or what ye shall drink; nor yet for your body, what ye shall put on. Is not the life more than the food, and the body than the raiment? Behold the birds of the heaven, that they sow not, neither do they reap, nor gather into barns; and your heavenly Father feedeth them. Are not ye of much more value then they? And which of you by being anxious can add one cubit unto the measure of his life?*
> MATTHEW 6:25-27

But seek ye first his kingdom, and his righteousness; and all these things shall be added unto you. Be not therefore anxious for the morrow: for the morrow will be anxious for itself. Sufficient unto the day is the evil thereof. MATTHEW 6:33 - 34

———————————— —∿— ————————————

SITUATION: While dating this guy, you go out of town for a friend's wedding. It's the wedding of the year, as those of high-society status will be there. You get to the hotel you will be staying at for the weekend. You run into the lobby to find your man with another woman. He wasn't expecting you until the next day. He plays it off by making a lame excuse and tells you that he'll see you later at the evening party, but doesn't show. On the day of the wedding, he acts like he's too busy to spend any time with you. Then, he asks you to ride back home with him after the festivities are all over and you do.

THOUGHT: How foolish can you be? This guy hasn't spent more than five minutes with you the entire weekend. He had his other woman with him for all the festivities before, during and after the wedding, and you still agreed to ride back home with him? Are you just Crazy or hard-up for a man? After you realized he was there with another woman, you should have given him his walking papers and went on and had a wonderful time with all the single brothers who were there trying to holla at you. Don't be passive- open your eyes and take off the rose-colored glasses.

How Would You Handle It?

_____

_____

_____

_____

What Does God's Word Say About It?

Yea, in the way of thy judgments, O Jehovah, have we waited for thee; to thy name, even to thy memorial name, is the desire of our soul. ISAIAH 26:8

Be not deceived; God is not mocked: for whatsoever a man soweth, that shall he also reap. GALATIANS 6:7

—☙—

SITUATION: You go to visit your boyfriend who's incarcerated and find out that his other woman is in line to see him as well. She confronts and tells you that she is his wife and that he told her to come and see him today. To add insult to injury, she says that she better be allowed the opportunity to see him, because she rode the bus all the way downtown for the trip. You are angry, to say the least, but wait to see if you will be allowed to visit him.

THOUGHT: Wow! Well, see what had happen was… How dumb of you to still be hanging on to this man, when he's neither married to you or her and had the nerve to ask you to come and see him, knowing that his other woman would be there. This is too much drama for me!

How Would You Handle It?

_____

_____

_____

_____

What Does God's Word Say About It?

> *Now the natural man receiveth not the things of the Spirit of God: for they are foolishness unto him; and he cannot know them, because they are spiritually judged.* I CORINTHIANS 2:14

> *Ye know this, my beloved brethren. But let every man be swift to hear, slow to speak, slow to wrath: for the wrath of man worketh not the righteousness of God.* JAMES 1:19-20

FANTASY

SITUATION: You're in a relationship with a much older man who approaches you about fulfilling his fantasy of having intimate experiences with multiple partners-him, you and another female. He expresses that he doesn't want you to do anything other than be a "receiver" from the other female, as it's his fantasy to see another female satisfy you. To make it more comfortable for you, he offers to cover all the expenses involved with the ordeal. He even says that the other female can be someone you know.

THOUGHT: Are you kidding me? Hopefully, you let him know that's not your cup of tea. Make it clear that you don't do multiple partners. Why would he expect you to partake in a perverse fantasy? Whatever happened to a fantasy with the two of you having an intimate time on the beach, under the moonlight? Don't try everything that comes to mind, because you just might like it-then you'll really have a problem on your hands!

How Would You Handle It?

_____

_____

_____

_____

What Does God's Word Say About It?

Let marriage be had in honor among all, and let the bed be undefiled: for fornicators and adulterers God will judge. HEBREWS 13:4

Thou shalt not commit adultery EXODUS 20:14

FRIENDSHIPS AND GIRLFRIENDS

SITUATION: Your car's in the shop, so you call your girlfriend whom you talk to daily, and ask if she can pick you up for rehearsal. She immediately asks if you can call another girlfriend to pick you up instead. Afterwards, she doesn't communicate with you for over two weeks, at which time she sends you a text asking why you didn't respond to her text. Huh?

THOUGHT: First things first: If this is your girl and she's unable to pick you up for whatever reason, she should be woman enough to say what the real problem is and not have asked you to call someone else instead. I'm sure you would have done that, anyway. It's so important to always be true to yourself and others if you want to have successful relationships. Being true sets the expectation of others and helps them to understand where you are coming from.

How Would You Handle It?

_____

_____

_____

_____

What Does God's Word Say About It?

> *For we take thought for things honorable, not only in the sight of the Lord, but also in the sight of men.* II CORINTHIANS 8:21

And if thy brother sin against thee, go, show him his fault between thee and him alone: if he hear thee, thou hast gained thy brother. But if he hear thee not, take with thee one or two more, that at the mouth of two witnesses or three every word may be established. And if he refuse to hear them, tell it unto the church: and if he refuse to hear the church also, let him be unto thee as the Gentile and the publican. MATTHEW 18:15-17

Finally, brethren, whatsoever things are true, whatsoever things are honorable, whatsoever things are just, whatsoever things are pure, whatsoever things are lovely, whatsoever things are of good report; if there be any virtue, and if there be any praise, think on these things. The things which ye both learned and received and heard and saw in me, these things do: and the God of peace shall be with you. PHILIPPIANS 4:8-9

NINETY-DAY WAITING PERIOD

SITUATION: In a new relationship, what is the time frame to express to your partner that you are in love or falling in love with them? The same question can be asked regarding when to engage in intimate relations with your partner for the first time and if there is an order to who initiates this intimacy.

THOUGHT: Well, in his book, Act Like A Lady, Think Like A Man, Steve Harvey says that there's a 90-day rule regarding the time frame before you "do the do" or "get it on." However, God's rule is very different and says that you shouldn't engage in sex until you are married. However, we are human and know that pre-marital sex occurs daily. It is recommended that you abstain if possible. As for when it's the best time to say "I Love You," don't say it until you're sure that you are in love with the person and not just infatuated, which is usually the case for most people today. I'm not one that falls in love fast, but when I do, I'm in love and I take it seriously. I want the person to know that I'm for real when I say it-those words are not just mere words to me.

How Would You Handle It?

_____

_____

_____

_____

What Does God's Word Say About It?

> *But, because of fornications, let each man have his own wife, and let each woman have her own husband.* I CORINTHIANS 7:2

> *But I say to the unmarried and to widows, It is good for them if they abide even as I. But if they have not continency, let them marry: for it is better to marry than to burn.* I CORINTHIANS 7:8-9

Part IV

"Mama Told Me There Would Be

Dayz Like This"

ABUSE—MENTALLY, PHYSICALLY, AND EMOTIONALLY
"Unforgiveness: Before You Move Forwrd, You Have To Forgive"

SITUATION: You have an emotional affair by opening up to a man, during a less-than-satisfying time in your marriage.

THOUGHT: It's so important in relationships to focus on the present and be active in the relationship you choose to be in. Having intimate conversations with a man who is not your husband can cause your mind and emotions to play tricks on you. It's so easy to think that the grass is greener on the other side. Emotional attachments can sometimes be just as bad as physical ones. Be careful not to confuse with what you actually need with what you want. You can have the same relationship that you're seeking with someone new, with your husband if you would just take the time to get to know him better. Yet, so many times, we discover this after the affair, which puts us back at square one. Like Brian McKnight's song Back at One says, "If ever I believe my work is done, then I start back at one."

How Would You Handle It?

_____

_____

_____

_____

What Does God's Word Say About It?

To him therefore that knoweth to do good, and doeth it not, to him it is sin. JAMES 4:17

———————————— —ɯ— ————————————

SITUATION: You were molested by your father for years. Your mother was an alcoholic and lady of the evening, so she wasn't there to take care of her responsibility to her husband and he chose the next best thing-you. You had to take care of your siblings and the house. As an adult, you feel that as a result of your molestation that you're not good enough for a decent relationship and still harbor the scars from your pain as a child.

THOUGHT: I am grateful to God that I was never subject to this insanity as a child, which makes it's hard to speak on it today, but I have many girlfriends who were subjected to this inhumane behavior by the hands of someone who they loved and trusted. I probably would still be kicking them in a place that would cause them pain internally, for the rest of their lives for the scars that they inflicted upon me. This type of behavior needs to be reported to parents immediately. Hopefully, the parents will address and stop it from happening. If the parents aren't responsible because they are trying to feed their own appetites, then the abuse must be reported to the law enforcement. Children are a blessing from God and should be protected from the hands of the enemy. Now, you have to forgive them for the harm they inflicted upon you before you can really move forward. You'll also need counseling, so you can have healthy and fulfilling relationships and feel good about who you. Most importantly, you'll need counseling to ensure you do not become an abuser yourself. Remember, forgiveness is not for them, it's for you.

How Would You Handle It?

_____

_____

_____

_____

What Does God's Word Say About It?

> *And whosoever shall cause one of these little ones that believe on me to stumble, it were better for him if a great millstone were hanged about his neck, and he were cast into the sea.* MARK 9:42

> *Train up a child in the way he should go, And even when he is old he will not depart from it.* PROVERBS 22:6

———————————————— —ᴡᴡ— ————————————————

SITUATION: Should I stay with my spouse who has developed a substance abuse problem? He lost his job and has been disruptive to our family life. He's no longer functioning as a capable parent.

THOUGHT: Oh, how my heart aches for these situations, as the whole family is effected by this type of behavior. This is so serious, because all are hurting; all have to see the father go through this sickness and watch him lose his self-respect and livelihood to such a crippling, debilitating disease. This man should seek counseling or help from a rehabilitation clinic. I would also recommend that all involved parties seek counseling to help them understand what their husband and father is going through. There are no right words to say to a child for what their parent is going through, so counseling is a necessity. If you are willing to stick it out and be there to support your husband, it is a great help to him because recovery is a lonely place without the support of family. The choice is up to you whether you choose to stay or leave, just make sure you and your loved ones are not in harm's way.

How Would You Handle It?

_____

_____

_____

_____

What Does God's Word Say About It?

Woe unto them that rise up early in the morning, that they may follow strong drink; that tarry late into the night, till wine inflame them! ISAIAH 5:11

Wherefore girding up the loins of your mind, be sober and set your hope perfectly on the grace that is to be brought unto you at the revelation of Jesus Christ. I PETER 1:13

Wives, be in subjection unto your own husbands, as unto the Lord.
For the husband is the head of the wife, and Christ also is the head
of the church, being himself the saviour of the body. EPHESIANS 5:22-23

But the fruit of the Spirit is love, joy, peace, long-suffering, kindness,
goodness, faithfulness, meekness, self-control; against such there is
no law. GALATIANS 5:22-23

SITUATION: You are dating a guy who doesn't go to church, doesn't like to be around your friends, and is very jealous. He does everything under the sun and is afraid that you'll find out. After an out-of-town trip with the choir you sing with, you see him while riding with your girlfriend but don't stop because you are going to get your car and come back. You come back, only to have him accuse you of all sorts of things like staying out all night and sleeping around. When you refuse to stay and listen to all that craziness and begin to drive off, he throws a rock and busts the window out of your car. After arriving home, your brother sees what has happened and wants to go hurt him, but you convince him not to. On another occasion, while at the library studying for your exams, this guy comes looking for you and accuses you of cheating on him. This time, he throws the assignment that you have been working on all day, out of the window and slaps you so hard, you see stars.

THOUGHT: Why is it that a man has the power to hit you so hard that you see stars, but with the same hands, can make the hairs stand up on the back of your head and bring you such pleasure by his touch? My mama always said, "If a man hits you once, he'll do it again." Domestic violence is never a safe place. Don't continue to stay and accept that type of behavior. Stop being a silent victim and let someone know what you're going through. Get the help you need to break free and be healed from the abuse of that relationship. Free yourself from the bondage that so easily beset you. Drop those rocks! Forgive, forget and move forward.

How Would You Handle It?

_____

_____

_____

_____

What Does God's Word Say About It?

> *Jehovah trieth the righteous; But the wicked and him that loveth violence his soul hateth.* PSALM 11:5

> *Let no corrupt speech proceed out of your mouth, but such as is good for edifying as the need may be, that it may give grace to them that hear. And grieve not the Holy Spirit of God, in whom ye were sealed unto the day of redemption. Let all bitterness, and wrath, and anger, and clamor, and railing, be put away from you, with all malice: and be ye kind one to another, tenderhearted, forgiving each other, even as God also in Christ forgave you.* EPHESIANS 4:29-32

SITUATION: You're dating someone who's abusing drugs and alcohol to the point of paranoia. He sees a car parked outside your house and accuses you of having another man at your house. When you advise that there's no one at your house, he drives by for several hours, then gets angry, stops and pulls a weapon out on you. You convince him that there's nobody in your house. He makes you get into the car with him and the two of you drive around until 7:00 a.m. in the morning. Then he drops you off at his mother's house and doesn't come back until 7:00 p.m. in the evening, drugged up and paranoid. He continues waving that weapon at you. You eventually call a family friend to pick you up.

THOUGHT: WOW, I would say that he was armed and extremely dangerous! You need to let that crazy and deranged fellow go on about his business with the quickness. Sometimes love will make you do crazy things. However, we need to be careful not to get hurt physically in the process. Praise God, you're still here to tell the story: First the test, then the testimony. Thank God for His protection. Learn from this experience and don't ever accept that type of behavior in another relationship. What's that Beyoncé says? "Your love's got me lookin so crazy right now. Looking so crazy in love's got me looking so crazy in love."

How Would You Handle It?

_____

_____

_____

_____

What Does God's Word Say About It?

Jehovah is my light and my salvation; Whom shall I fear? Jehovah is the strength of my life; Of whom shall I be afraid? PSALMS 27:1

In thee, O Jehovah, do I take refuge; Let me never be put to shame: Deliver me in thy righteousness. PSALMS 31:1

GENERAL RELATIONSHIP ISSUES

SITUATION: Would you agree to be "the other woman" in a relationship where a brother tells you that he's going back to his ex-wife, but every chance he gets, he's trying to get with you for a quickie? Following, he finds a reason to leave, says he's coming back but doesn't.

THOUGHT: Can't you see that all this brother wants is the goods and nothing else? You're not important to him at all-it's just sex to him. If you continue to allow him to see you on the side, then that's what he'll continue to do. You have to stop the madness. Let him know that out of respect for yourself, you're not just going to accept that behavior. No matter how good it is, don't except anything less than what you're worth. If nothing else, you need somebody to hold you after it's all said and done. Stop wasting your time with someone else's man. Don't be stuck on stupid all your natural-born life. He might consider being your man if you stop accepting that foolishness because a man wants a challenge. No Pain, No Gain!

How Would You Handle It?

_____

_____

_____

_____

What Does God's Word Say About It?

> *For what doth it profit a man, to gain the whole world, and forfeit his life?* MARK 8:36

SITUATION: You receive a call from an old flame fishing around to see if you are dating and when you tell him that you're not going to discuss your personal life with him, he has the nerve to say, "Well, you go out and date around if you want to, but I know you'll be back." What in the world? When you ask him how he figures that, he says, "Because they always come back. Women leave me and then realize I was better than what's out there and they come back." After your head stops spinning from his audacity, you reassure him you won't be coming back. Can you believe this guy?

THOUGHT: Well, I can appreciate the confidence in this brotha. He must really be putting it down, if a sistah always comes back. And if they do come back, then why is he calling you to see if you're dating or not. I think he realizes that he's the one who missed out and wants you back. If he was so great, then why did you leave him in the first place? Maybe he's just having a moment. It also sounds like he's a little full of himself- maybe that's why you left him to begin with!

How Would You Handle It?

_____

_____

_____

_____

What Does God's Word Say About It?

> *Every one that is proud in heart is an abomination to Jehovah: Though hand join in hand, he shall not be unpunished.* PROVERBS 16:5

> *Seest thou a man wise in his own conceit? There is more hope of a fool than of him.* ROVERBS 26:12

SITUATION: You're single, but you're not. There are days when you invite God over for breakfast and ask Him just how many more nights you will spend alone. This is where checking your self-esteem comes in to play. It's important that you find yourself worthy of someone who will care about and treat you the way God created you to be treated. First, you have to stop just knowing better and start doing better. That begins with trusting God's plan for your life. You think that if you wait on God to send you a good man, you'll be waiting forever because there aren't that many good men out there-wrong! A good man may need to be told "no," but if he is getting "yes" all of the time, he may never rise to the occasion. Instead of thinking you have to compete with the many women out there, learn how to set your standards and stick to them. You know the old saying, "If you don't some other woman will?" I say, "Then let her." I had a man actually tell me that he wasn't interested in getting married. His exact words were, "Baby I'm not looking for ownership, I just want to rent." Can you believe that? When a guy tells you that he's only interested in keeping you around for his need and pleasure without a commitment, don't settle! The real problem was that I had been renting myself out all along and never getting the right occupier who would take care of what had been entrusted to them. Yes, I'm using an analogy about renting and home ownership but after it was proposed to me, I had to really think about what that statement was saying. You can choose to be a temporary situation or a long term situation-it's up to you to decide.

THOUGHT: In life we have to learn how to be in love with ourselves under God's care. He loves you the most, He wants you to be your best, and He takes the mess of your life and makes it good for His purpose and plan. It's funny how we discover this after we've been used and abused by someone who never meant us any good to begin with. We are always looking for a place to park our heart. I'm a firm believer that we arrive at that place when God sets us free from the bondage that has kept us captive for so long. At that point, we're freed to go on and live, love and laugh for God Almighty-the only man who really gets the glory out of your life. He knows all about you and loves you just the same. The best thing about Him is that He'll never ever, leave you or forsake you; He'll be with you until the end of time. Now, why don't you try loving Him back, with your whole heart, mind, body and soul? I'm confident that He'll know how to receive it, and He will treat you right-no doubt about it!

How Would You Handle It?

_____

_____

_____

_____

What Does God's Word Say About It?

When thou passest through the waters, I will be with thee; and through the rivers, they shall not overflow thee: when thou walkest through the fire, thou shalt not be burned, neither shall the flame kindle upon thee. ISAIAH 43:2

SITUATION: You're dating an ex-military solder that's very fresh with the ladies. He strikes up conversations, gets their numbers, but never shares this information with you. He doesn't normally go places like church, etc with you, but normally arrives at those places after you have arrived or left in order to see and hangout with your female associates. They are always referring to him in conversation with you in ways that indicates he hangs out with them a lot. He even called you after you guys break up and leaves a morbid message that your deceased mother had called; only for you to find out that one of the female associates from the church knew about it. How do you handle this situation???

THOUGHT: SURELY this person is so far out of your life that you can't remember what he looks like or his name for that matter.....what a horrible thing to do as to calling and leaving a message that your deceased mother called and left a message for you to call her back. Now, how is that possible, and I would still be looking for the "witch" that was in on it today, for a butt whipping. CLEARLY, she was NO friend or associate of yours; how dirty and conniving she had to be to agree on a prank such as that. Unfortunately we meet people who mean us no earthy good right off the bat; this appeared to be just that type of person; he just probably needed a place to hang out when he was visiting your city and you fit the bill. He obviously had no intentions of seriously dating you from the get go, especially since he was so liberal with giving his number out and flirting with the women in your circle or chu'ch; did he not think it wouldn't get back to you by one of them. UGGH!!!

How Would You Handle It?

_____

_____

_____

_____

What Does God's Word Say About It?

But I say, walk by the Spirit, and ye shall not fulfil the lust of the flesh. For the flesh lusteth against the Spirit, and the Spirit against the flesh; for these are contrary the one to the other; that ye may not do the things that ye would. But if ye are led by the Spirit, ye are not under the law. Now the works of the flesh are manifest, which are these: fornication, uncleanness, lasciviousness, idolatry, sorcery, enmities, strife, jealousies, wraths, factions, divisions, parties, envyings, drunkenness, revellings, and such like; of which I forewarn you, even as I did forewarn you, that they who practise such things shall not inherit the kingdom of God. But the fruit of the Spirit is love, joy, peace, longsuffering, kindness, goodness, faithfulness, meekness, self-control; against such there is no law. And they that are of Christ Jesus have crucified the flesh with the passions and the lusts thereof. If we live by the Spirit, by the Spirit let us also walk. Let us not become vainglorious, provoking one another, envying one another. GALATIANS 5:16-26

SITUATION: You meet this guy in your complex, you know he's watching you, has been for many days now, but doesn't say anything to you. Finally he gets around to it and asks if you are dating anyone, your reply, no. He looks fairly young, so you ask how old he was; his reply 34 fix-in-to be 35; what GROWN man says that? That was an immediate turn off for you as you're 47 and has a daughter almost his age. He insists that he's old enough and knows how to treat a woman. You have a couple of conversations with him just to see, and just as you thought, his conversations were very engaging for the "Young and the Restless" as the first time he called and you were not available his response was, "I called you several times and you didn't return my call, that made me very angry." Need I say more...That substantiates my earlier statement.

THOUGHT: It's so important to separate the Boyz from the Men; and you must do that quickly. All women aren't Cougars; some do want the luxury of spending their time with a GROWN MAN!!! I would have ran and not looked back when he said he was 34 fix-in-to-be 35, yeah you're right what GROWN Man says that, then tries to convince you that he's old enough and knows how to treat a woman. My question would have been have you ever been with a GROWN Woman b4??? Then I would have most likely passed and not entertained that young Man. And the fact that you have a daughter almost his age would have CLEARLY been another turn-off for me. Young bloods like this tend to have a problem with you not being at their beck-and-call when they're trying to reach you as well, don't need nobody peeping me like that; and they tend to be foolish, jealous and have very bad understandings. I'll PASS TOO!!! A note to the wise, if you're calling the man in your life a boyfriend, then that's exactly what you'll get, a boy. A man should be addressed as a Man, and not a boy out of respect. There is a distinctive difference; if you didn't know, now you know.

How Would You Handle It?

_____

_____

_____

_____

What Does God's Word Say About It?

> *There is precious treasure and oil in the dwelling of the wise; But a foolish man swalloweth it up.* PROVERBS 21:20

> *But if any of you lacketh wisdom, let him ask of God, who giveth to all liberally and upbraideth not; and it shall be given him.* JAMES 1:5

SITUATION: An individual has been involved with the man in her life for over six years now, but refuses to take the relationship to the next level because of certain situations with her son who has gotten into trouble repeatedly. Somehow she feels embarrassed by his behavior and is unwilling to share this information with the man in her life.

THOUGHT: Six years is a long time to be involved with someone and not be married to them. As it relates to her children, she's not allowing him to be active in her affairs if she's not willing to openly share what's going on in her life, which is unfair to him as well as the relationship. When you're involved with a person that long, you shouldn't pick and choose what you want to discuss and what you don't want to discuss. I'm sure he has some idea of what's going on if you've been together that long anyway. Children are going to be children, your responsibility is to teach and raise them up the best way possible by instilling good values and principles; the decisions they make will affect them afterwards, not you or your relationships if you handle them correctly. It's not always a good thing to be so involved in our children's lives where it rubs off on your relationship with your significant other. Another reason to discuss with him, as he might be able to offer a better solution to the existing problems from a male's perspective; sometimes males relate better to males. What do you have to lose; two heads are always better than one.

How Would You Handle It?

_____

_____

_____

_____

What Does God's Word Say About It?

Faithful is the saying: For if we died with him, we shall also live with him: if we endure, we shall also reign with him: if we shall deny him, he also will deny us: if we are faithless, he abideth faithful; for he cannot deny himself. Of these things put them in remembrance, charging them in the sight of the Lord, that they strive not about words, to no profit, to the subverting of them that hear. Give diligence to present thyself approved unto God, a workman that needeth not to be ashamed, handling aright the word of truth. I TIMOTHY 2:11-15

SITUATION: You've been dating and living with a man for over two years, and finds out by one of the women that he's been messing around with that he's been seeing her on a regular basis. You confront the brother; he not only denies it, but gets mad with you for talking to the other woman about his relationship with her. The other woman tells you about trips that they have taken together, money she's spent on him and how he plans to leave you for her. The problem here is the apartment you live in and vehicles that you drive all belong to him. Do you continue to stay and drive his vehicles and live in the place in his name or do you give it all up and branch out on your own???

THOUGHT: If you wait long enough people will show you themselves. I'm sure you must be hurt; two years is a long time to give of yourself to another person in a relationship; sometimes love isn't fair, you have to express your feelings about the situation, then pick yourself up and move on; unless you decide to stay there and work through that pain. You will get past it, but the fact of the matter is you still have to go through that painful feeling; let nobody tell you how you should handle it. Pray and ask GOD to help you get through it. I would definitely let him know what a dirty low-down person he's been for not being true enough to tell you the truth after the cat was out of the bag. As for the other woman, she wanted you to be hurt, I would discontinue any conversations with her as well; she's already done the damage she meant to do. Mama always said that it's better to have your own stuff and be able to take care of your own self. You should always be prepared for a rainy day, as sure as the sun is shinning, they will come. Shacking up is never a good place to be in either.

How Would You Handle It?

_____

_____

_____

_____

What Does God's Word Say About It?

For all have sinned, and fall short of the glory of God. ROMANS 3:23

For if ye forgive men their trespasses, your heavenly Father will also forgive you. But if ye forgive not men their trespasses, neither will your Father forgive your trespasses. MATTHEW 6:14-15

———————————— —☿— ————————————

SITUATION: Several women have expressed that during the courtship stages their boyfriends/husbands would open the doors, pull out the chairs, compliment them on their dress, hair, etc; but after about 6-12 months into the relationship stop doing those things and get angry when it's brought up, or they only do it because it's brought up then it stops.

THOUGHT: I'm a firm believer of the same thing it took to get the person is the same thing you need to do to keep them. Chivalry is not dead; there are still men out there who want to wine and dine you; that have the ultimate courteous behavior towards women. We as women need to let them know that we appreciate the treatment. I don't think there's anything wrong with bringing the subject up to your spouse, man, or significant other if for nothing else to see why he felt it was important then, but not as important now that he's conquered and gotten you. I personally will ask them not to do anything during the courtship that they aren't planning to keep up in the marriage. That's the reason relationships are failing today, because we stop courting and making our partners feel special; instead we would rather do it for someone else that we've only known for a minute or two. Relationships are like old vintage wine, they get better with time, if preserved properly. We need to stop and take the time to value and appreciate what we already have; water your own garden to ensure it grows. I have a friend who's Aunt/Uncle still hold hands after 30 years of marriage. Her husband still opens the door and pulls out the chair for her today. I also recall recently sitting next to, what I would call a seasoned couple at church one Sunday, and the entire time her husband held and caressed her hands the entire service, I thought that was priceless. I believe there's still hope for this lost generation, if they take note.

How Would You Handle It?

_____

_____

_____

_____

What Does God's Word Say About It?

Husbands, love your wives, even as Christ also loved the church, and gave himself up for it; that he might sanctify it, having cleansed it by the washing of water with the word, that he might present the church to himself a glorious church, not having spot or wrinkle or any such thing; but that it should be holy and without blemish. Even so ought husbands also to love their own wives as their own bodies. He that loveth his own wife loveth himself: for no man ever hated his own flesh; but nourisheth and cherisheth it, even as Christ also the church. EPHESIANS 5:25-29

But the fruit of the Spirit is love, joy, peace, long-suffering, kindness, goodness, faithfulness, meekness, self-control; against such there is no law. GALATIANS 5:22-23

SITUATION: You're in a real situation, I mean a REAL situation. You have been talking to this guy for approximately a year and a half; the only reason the two of you haven't gotten together sexually is because the two of you live in two difference states. You share a lot, and you're there mentally for one another. The mental connection is so deep that he can arouse you over the phone like none other. Problem is, he's involved in a committed relationship in the city where he lives, but they don't connect mentally in the same capacity that you and he does. You know, they are cool, but he's able to talk with you about things he could never talk to her about; she actually would look at him differently if he asked

"Life's Little Lessons - GOOD, bad, or InDiFfErEnT
That Get You from Here to There"

her to mentally arouse him over the phone, that's just not what she does; no disrespect to her. To add a little more flavor to the mix, you are now involved with someone that you're really feeling, which is taking away from those late night phone calls.

THOUGHT: Once you connect with a man mentally and emotionally, you're half way there and when the two meets up with the physical, it's an EARTHQUAKE!!! Whatever you want you can get, sistah. If I had to describe it, it's like the curling of toes; it blows that brotha's mind and lets him know he has just arrived at that place where he finds himself walking around the office saying "GOOD MORNIN!!!" to everybody, just skinning and grinning, like a Cheshire Cat. And it's just as important to let a sistah know that she has taken you there. That's when you're both on Cloud 9. It's like those lyrics from that Temptations' song – "I Can't Get next To You:" - I can turn a gray sky blue. I can make it rain, whenever I wanted to. Oh, I - I can build a castle from a single grain of sand. I can make a ship sail, uh, on dry land. But my life is incomplete and I'm so blue. 'Cause I can't get next to you. Now you know I do have to bring you back to reality; I recommend that the both of you think about the other individuals in your lives and if you can't be with the one you love, go on and love the one you're with, in hopes that they will make you feel the way you make one another feel.

How Would You Handle It?

_____

_____

_____

_____

What Does God's Word Say About It?

For the word of God is living, and active, and sharper than any two-edged sword, and piercing even to the dividing of soul and spirit, of both joints and marrow, and quick to discern the thoughts and intents of the heart. HEBREWS 4:12

SITUATION: While out with the girls on a Friday night you all meet some guys; go back to your friend's house have breakfast and good times, like you use to do during college days. You all couple off and end up staying the night together, however, nothing happens. You and the guy you met ends up liking one another and keep in touch over time. He moves away but the two of you continue to maintain a great connection, which ends up being 2 years or better. You realize that you are falling for him mentally, and would love to have a physical connection, but distance has kept you apart. You share openly with him, and he with you, but you agree to not get together sexually because it would be too EXPLOSIVE if the two of you connected; at this point and feel the friendship is more important. To top it all off, he's involved in a committed relationship with his lady of 3 years, he admits to you that he's in love with her. Should you continue talking to this man, and sharing your innermost desires and dreams; would you consider this a form of cheating???

THOUGHT: Sometimes in life you meet a person and the timing's all off...You say to yourself, "self" I wish I had met this person 6 months earlier, etc. Life's sometimes just isn't fair, why is it that you can meet a person while you're in a relationship and not be able to share the love the two of you have for one another. It's like fate never allowing the two of you to be together. The both of you fight like crazy to be apart because you know the chemistry's too strong. How long can you do that, is it selfish to not connect, or just continue to be apart, knowing he's the one for you and you're the one for him. Yes, it is a form of cheating if he's sharing things with you that he's not sharing with the person he's committed to and in love with. Even though this person gives you attention, he's still wrong for sharing things with you that he doesn't share with his lady. He really should be focusing on his relationship since he's still with her, to see how he can work out whatever problems they have. If he wanted to be with you no matter how important the friendship or distance between the two of you; he would have done it by now. There is a reason why he's still with her…he must be doing something right…hmmmmmmm!!! Cut your losses, if any and move on, as long as he's still with her, he can never be committed to you the way you would like.

How Would You Handle It?

_____

_____

_____

_____

What Does God's Word Say About It?

> *And he said unto them, It is not for you to know times or seasons, which the Father hath set within His own authority.* ACTS 1:7

SITUATION: Why it is that you wait and wait and wait for the right guy to come alone and when he does, all the "heathens" come out of the woodwork wanting to be with you; calling you all times of the day and night trying to get back with you?

THOUGHT: Misery loves company; if he didn't appreciate what he had in you when he was with you, then it's his lost. What's that they say, "Too bad, too sad"; now he's probably calling and telling you how much he misses and wants to be with you. Don't fall for that, it's the oldest trick in the book. Instead, focus on that brother who appreciates and treats you like the Queen you are. Hats off to him for recognizing what he now has. I wouldn't entertain the thought of seeing this other person any longer.

How Would You Handle It?

_____

_____

_____

_____

What Does God's Word Say About It?

> *Ye did not choose me, but I chose you, and appointed you, that ye should go and bear fruit, and that your fruit should abide: that whatsoever ye shall ask of the Father in my name, he may give it you.* JOHN 15:16

> *Even as he chose us in him before the foundation of the world, that we should be holy and without blemish before him in love.*
> EPHESIANS 1:4

SITUATION: You're dating a new guy; you both agreed to take it slow. You're excited about him being a stand up kind of guy. He's coming out of a newly divorced relationship, and have mentioned many times to take it slow because he's still dealing with some issues from his divorce, but doesn't call it off between the two of you. He's present, and the two of you see one another occasionally, But you really want to know if the relationship is going anywhere; and you know how you are, if you don't spend enough personal and quality time together with the person, you're begin to get bored, and could possibly move on. What do you do at this point???

THOUGHT: Rome wasn't built in a day; if you like the guy and he holds your interest a little bit then you should be willing to wait until he works out his issues from his divorce; the fact that he mentioned that to you is a good thing, especially since men don't usually share what's going on with them personally right off, so he must really like or have some feelings for you to even be sharing that much. On the other hand if you know that you're not able to wait then you need to be honest enough and let him know where you are and what your expectations are. What's meant to be will be, that's for sure. Men come a dime a dozens, but GOOD SINGLE ONES, are hard to find, so you might want to sit back and wait for this "brotha" to get him self together. What's that your Mama or Grandma use to say; "You're to hot for your own pants, you're beginning to smell yourself." You might be entertaining your husband and not know it.

How Would You Handle It?

_____

_____

_____

_____

What Does God's Word Say About It?

> *But they that wait for Jehovah shall renew their strength; they shall mount up with wings as eagles; they shall run, and not be weary; they shall walk, and not faint.* ISAIAH 40:31

———————————— ∽ ————————————

SITUATION: You're in a new relationship with a man that has the qualities that you seek; he's tall, dark n' handsome, bald, gainfully employed, not afraid of commitment or communication, is present; you feel good in his presence, and he's good at encouraging your efforts. He's just generally concern with your well being; not to mention that he gives it to you on a regular basis and it's good, but you don't feel that WOW factor yet.

THOUGHT: The question has been asked more than once, why does one person make you feel better than another person? Why is it that the "Bad Boyz" brings it better than anyone else in the whole United

States of America? But, a decent, hardworking man just doesn't always cut it. "It's hard out here for a PIMP...." We as women want so many things.....We want them good, but bad to the bones in the bed; We want them employed, but available to be with us as often as we like. Actually, it's a good thing that you're not all over the place with this person in this relationship, at this time; sounds like he's a very mature individual. You sound pretty confident that he's doing the right things, not to mention that he's giving it to you on the regular, and it's good!!! I recommend you sit back, relax, and enjoy learning more about the person, who knows, as you get to know him better he may present more of a WOW factor than you could have ever imagined. You can't always judge a book by its cover; the findings and discovery may be more rewarding than you ever thought. Keep reading my sister, keep reading; don't be deceived, you'll know if what you feel is right or good for you. Always follow your heart as it will never lead you wrong. God always sends you confirmation.

How Would You Handle It?

_____

_____

_____

_____

What Does God's Word Say About It?

The thief cometh not, but that he may steal, and kill, and destroy: I came that they may have life, and may have it abundantly.

JOHN 10:10

SITUATION: You divorce your wife of 1-1/2 years for irreconcilable differences during the breakup; she keeps some or all of your stuff; stuff that you had long before the two of you met; stuff that wouldn't do her any good and she refuses to give the stuff back to you, the rightful owner.

THOUGHT: My 1st thought was, why is she keeping his stuff, what's her plans for it. Who does that??? I consider this type of woman a bitter and very controlling person. That mentality that says, "If I can't have him no one else will, and I'll make his life miserable by keeping his stuff." This is a selfish and sick individual, who's better off by themselves than in a relationship. It's a good thing you got out of that relationship before it killed your emotions, self-esteem, and possibly have you wanting to do something to her. We as women need to learn to speak life into our relationships and into our MEN. For some brother's when it's over it's over. Let it go Poopalicious!!!

How Would You Handle It?

_____

_____

_____

_____

What Does God's Word Say About It?

> *Let all bitterness, and wrath, and anger, and clamor, and railing, be put away from you, with all malice: and be ye kind one to another, tenderhearted, forgiving each other, even as God also in Christ forgave you.* EPHESIANS 4:31-32

A soft answer turneth away wrath; But a grievous word stirreth up anger. PROVERBS 15:1

If a man say, I love God, and hateth his brother, he is a liar: for he that loveth not his brother whom he hath seen, cannot love God whom he hath not seen. I JOHN 4:20

—⁂—

SITUATION: You're in a relationship, things are going well; the person tells you that they have fallen in love with you; I mean like fallen hard, but you don't have that same love for them. You express that you like and have feelings for them but not in love with them. You are then asked if you had ever been in love before and if so with whom. After sharing, the person is crushed that you didn't have the same feelings for them. To the point that they almost can't handle it;

THOUGHT: Some things are not meant to be shared, as everyone can't handle the truth. You should tread lightly when you're dealing with an individual who may have been hurt badly in previous relationships. You might want to explain that you don't fall in love easily, but that you enjoy their company and continue to do things that could bring you closer and possibly even grow to love them. If it gets too much for them to handle you might want to suggest counseling for the person to be able to move forward and it not become so damaging for them.

How Would You Handle It?

_____

_____

_____

_____

What Does God's Word Say About It?

In nothing be anxious; but in everything by prayer and supplication with thanksgiving let your requests be made known unto God. And the peace of God, which passeth all understanding, shall guard your hearts and your thoughts in Christ Jesus. Finally, brethren, whatsoever things are true, whatsoever things are honorable, whatsoever things are just, whatsoever things are pure, whatsoever things are lovely, whatsoever things are of good report; if there be any virtue, and if there be any praise, think on these things.
PHILIPPIANS 4:6-8

—◊—

SITUATION: You meet a guy on a "social-networking" dating site; you like him a lot, and things are going well; due to the both of you meeting on this site, it could present a trust issue, especially since the two of you continue to log on daily; he confides that he met and married his previous wife on the same site. Is this a "red flag" for you?

THOUGHT: This could be a potential "red flag" however, it is about being honest with one another; I mean you met one another on a social-networking dating site, need I say more. I'm not saying that you can't make a love connection after meeting there, that's totally up to the two of you, millions do it daily. There are actually some weirdo's out there, we pray he's not. Especially since this is the wave of the future; you have to trust one another, until either gives the reason not too. There could be many reasons why the two of you continue to log into this site, discuss those reasons. Nothing beats communication; if it's expressed that you would rather the other person not continue communicating on this site and the problem still exist, then there's a bigger fish to fry. The fact that he was honest enough to let you know that he met and married someone from that site was a good thing. If nothing else you can respect the honesty. Give it a try; that's the only way to see if it's going to work or not. If it's meant to be, it'll be.

How Would You Handle It?

_____

_____

_____

_____

What Does God's Word Say About It?

> _Trust in Jehovah with all thy heart, And lean not upon thine own understanding._ PROVERBS 3:5

Therefore I say unto you, All things whatsoever ye pray and ask for, believe that ye receive them, and ye shall have them. MARK 11:24

—◊—

SITUATION: You meet this guy at a club; you both are feeling one another; you give him your number, a couple of days goes by; he calls and confides in you that he killed someone. The incident happened sometime ago; someone else was convicted of the crime. What do I do?

THOUGHT: OMG! Run Baby Run! Now, that's carrying a heavy load. Hopefully you didn't tell him where you live too. Just like online there are weirdo's also in the clubs. Maybe he needed someone to just talk too and you appealed to his softer side in that manner. Hopefully you were able to encourage him to repent, turn himself in and free the wrongfully accused person. I would also slowly but surely discontinue any further contact with this person if at all possible, and pray that he makes the right decision by tuning himself in.

How Would You Handle It?

_____

_____

_____

_____

What Does God's Word Say About It?

Then came Peter and said to him, Lord, how oft shall my brother sin against me, and I forgive him? until seven times? Jesus saith unto him, I say not unto thee, Until seven times; but, Until seventy times seven. MATTHEW 18:21-22

Forbearing one another, and forgiving each other, if any man have a complaint against any; even as the Lord forgave you, so also do ye.. COLOSSIANS 3:13

Thou shalt not kill. EXODUS 20:13

—⚬—

SITUATION: Why does it always feel like you are a cheap date when a man comes over to your place and leaves before the clock strikes twelve, but they want you to stay over night when you go to theirs??? And they always use a common excuse like, my cell phone is dead or I need to get home so I can get to bed, got to get up early in the morning, etc.

THOUGHT: Ah Hello!!! – you're probably already in bed.....It just goes to show you that Men are from Mars and Women are from Venus. They are visual and we are emotional. I guess we could view it in one of three ways; (1) They are respecting you and not staying because of how it looks to your neighbors; (2) They feel uncomfortable because of previous relationships where an unexpected visitor may have showed up unannounced or feel more secure and protective when you stay over their house; or (3) Their cell phone really is dead and they are expecting an important phone call. You be the judge, or just ask them why is it that they won't stay overnight at your place. I believe in asking the questions that I need answers too.....that's the best way. I was always told that there are no stupid or bad questions. It's the one not asked that I have a problem with.

How Would You Handle It?

_____

_____

_____

_____

What Does God's Word Say About It?

Let not then your good be evil spoken of. ROMAN: 14:16

———————————— ⁓⚬⁓ ————————————

SITUATION: You enter into a relationship with a person who's fresh out of a divorce; but has been separated for over 9 months. He's still damage goods, but is willing to take it slow with the relationship between the two of you. Is it good to be in this place at this time, or is it best to wait until the person has had the time to heal from the wounds of the past.

THOUGHT: I believe anything can be worked through if two agree. The first thought was to say no, wait until the person is healed. As long as the person is mature and is working on resolving those past wounds and their not continuing to have contact with the ex-spouse they should be ok. Communication would be the key to the longevity of this relationship and where it goes if you agreed to continue to date this person. I know for a fact that "hurting people hurt other people." Take it slow and keep GOD present on the forefront of everything. It's not good for the two of you to get physical to soon during this time. It's actually recommended that you give yourself at least 6 months before getting involved into a serious or committed relationship following a divorce, or any other separation for that matter. It would also be good for him to seek counseling to assist with healing some of those deep-rooted wounds. The first place to begin your healing is within yourself; from there you can help someone else. It starts with you, when you see the truth, accept and forgive, then you're on the way to recovery; that's the time to fully move on with your new life. You gotta keep the FAITH.

How Would You Handle It?

_____

_____

_____

_____

What Does God's Word Say About It?

> *Thou shalt not take vengeance, nor bear any grudge against the children of thy people; but thou shalt love thy neighbor as thyself: I am Jehovah.* LEVITICUS 19:18

And forgive us our debts, as we also have forgiven our debtors.
MATTHEW 6:12

Jehovah is nigh unto them that are of a broken heart, And saveth such as are of a contrite spirit. PSALM 34:18

Remember ye not the former things, neither consider the things of old. II CORINTHIANS 1:3-4

Blessed be the God and Father of our Lord Jesus Christ, the Father of mercies and God of all comfort; who comforteth us in all our affliction, that we may be able to comfort them that are in any affliction, through the comfort wherewith we ourselves are comforted of God. ISAIAH 43:18

Now the God of hope fill you with all joy and peace in believing, that ye may abound in hope, in the power of the Holy Spirit. ROMAN 15:13

—m—

SITUATION: You were married and the marriage ended up in a divorce due to infidelity, is the one who committed the infidelity, in the eyes of God or according to scripture, able to marry again?

THOUGHT: This is the #1 question of the day; if I get divorced, can I remarry, and if so, will it bring adultery upon the person that I remarry. The basic rule is that divorce and remarriage are not permitted, except for adultery or desertion, and that is the rule the church should stick to. When adultery has taken place, a divorce can be obtained, because adultery has already severed the marriage relationship and divorce is a formal acknowledgment of what has already taken place. There are certain instances in which divorce and remarriage are permitted without the remarriage being considered adultery. These instances would include unrepentant adultery, physical abuse of spouse or children, and abandonment of a believing spouse by an unbelieving spouse. I'm not saying that a person under such circumstances should remarry. The Bible definitely encourages remaining single or reconciliation. At the same time, it is my understanding that God offers His mercy and grace to the innocent party in a divorce and allows that person to remarry without it being considered adultery. There are repercussions, but God can restore.

Remarks from Chief Servant V.L. Young: Now that you know and are listening to God's word, if this be the case, and if you have confessed that you did sin in divorcing and you sincerely repent, and you sincerely want to go forward and not make that sin again, then God forgives you, it is done, you are forgiven and now it is time to get right and not repeat the sin. That is the key here, "Go and sin no more!!!" which means do not break another covenant you have made! So, God does honor the marriage covenant you are in now, because it is a covenant and He expects you to stop sinning, do not repeat the sin again, to divorce again is even worse because you are not only committing the sin of divorce, you are committing the sin of iniquity as well.

As a footnote from CBN.com: The church should use its power of "binding and loosing" (see Matthew 16:19) to provide guidance in the way of forgiveness to divorced and remarried couples who have received Jesus Christ after their divorce. In other words, the church should (and I personally would) say that what happened in your past life is covered by the blood of Christ. Enjoy your present marriage and live in it to the glory of God without recrimination. However, for Christians who have divorced (after being born again) for reasons other than adultery or desertion, I believe they should either be reconciled to their Christian mates or remain unmarried.

How Would You Handle It?

What Does God's Word Say About It? ?

> *Verily I say unto you, what things soever ye shall bind on earth shall be bound in heaven; and what things soever ye shall loose on earth shall be loosed in heaven.* MATTHEW 18:18

> *And we know that to them that love God all things work together for good, even to them that are called according to his purpose.*
> ROMANS 8:28

> *Read entire chapter.* I CORINTHIANS 7

> *Wherefore if any man is in Christ, he is a new creature: the old things are passed away; behold, they are become new.*
> II CORINTHIANS 5:17

*And I say unto you, Whosoever shall put away his wife, except for
fornication, and shall marry another, committeth adultery: and
he that marrieth her when she is put away committeth adultery.*

MATTHEW 19:9

SITUATION: Individual has been single for a long time and decided
to marry someone who they once dated in the past. The reason for the
separation in the past was that the person chose to marry someone
else. Upon moving back to the city the person calls to advise their back
and want to reconcile with you. The reconciliation takes place and you
immediately move the person in and begin working on the relationship.
In doing so, you see some imperfections which are not properly
addressed. You later get married and the REAL problems begin. Things
like excessive spending and drinking, as well as other things that were
accepted but never addressed before the marriage.

THOUGHT: "The way you start a relationship is the way it's going to
continue." Don't do things while you're dating that you're not going
to maintain after marriage. If you allow certain things to occur in your
relationship and don't properly address them, that's the way it's going
to continue; which ultimately sets you up for failure, and confuses the
other person, simply because you accepted it before and now that you're
married it's a problem. It's so important to communicate your wants,
needs and desires to your partner so they clearly understand what your
expectations are before marriage. A marriage automatically comes with

its own share of problems, so why add unwanted complications to them. As an adult you should be able to communicate to the other person your likes and dislikes. Uh Oh....I guess I should have said mature adults, there is a difference. An added note from a woman of wisdom, my Nanny; "If you live with a person before marriage, you have already allowed Satan the opportunity to destroy your marriage before it starts.....it'll never be right from that point on." Only God can change that thing after the fact, rely and trust him to bring it to past. If your marriage is truly important to you seek marriage guidance or counseling.

How Would You Handle It?

_____

_____

_____

_____

What Does God's Word Say About It?

And I say unto you, Ask, and it shall be given you; seek, and ye shall find; knock, and it shall be opened unto you. LUKE 11:9

And whatsoever ye shall ask in my name, that will I do, that the Father may be glorified in the Son. JOHN 14:13

For this is the will of God, even your sanctification, that ye abstain from fornication; that each one of you know how to possess himself of his own vessel in sanctification and honor, not in the passion of lust, even as the Gentiles who know not God. I THESSALONIANS 4:3-5

MISC...

SITUATION: Often times it feels like our lives mirror a box of chocolates. We take chances on the many flavors; some taste good and when they do, we keep on chewing; the ones that taste bad, we spit out immediately, just so we can take another bite of something better, and we keep on trying until the box is empty, in hopes of getting the right ones. I'm glad God doesn't treat us as a box of valentine chocolates, but as a bee that produces honey from the sweetness of the honey comb.

THOUGHT: "Life is like a box of chocolates, you never know what you're going to get." like that famous quote from Forrest Grump. Yeah, Life is like a box of assorted chocolates, loaded with surprises, some good and some bad. Yummy when their good; so we search for more just like it, and yucky when their bad; very hard on the taste buds. Those yucky ones, however, determine our depth of character. If life was all good, and your faith was never tested, where would you be spiritually? It's the bad times that test our faith and cause us to mature as we learn to rely on God for everything we've been through. Praise God for those times, as they come to make us strong, and birth us for our testimonies which ultimately help someone else; although we can't see that as we're going through. "We are tested to birth a testimony for someone else to learn from." Lord, help us to see your will in all of the seasons of our lives. Help us to remember that there is a time for everything and that your timing is always the right timing. The one constant thing is and will always be YOU, as you never change. Your name is the same, today and forevermore.

How Would You Handle It?

_____

_____

_____

_____

What Does God's Word Say About It?

> _Now it came to pass on the day when the sons of God came to present themselves before Jehovah, that Satan also came among them. And Jehovah said unto Satan, Whence comest thou? Then Satan answered Jehovah, and said, From going to and fro in the earth, and from walking up and down in it. And Jehovah said unto Satan, Hast thou considered my servant Job? for there is none like him in the earth, a perfect and an upright man, one that feareth God, and turneth away from evil. Then Satan answered Jehovah, and said, Doth Job fear God for nought? Hast not thou made a hedge about him, and about his house, and about all that he hath, on every side? Thou hast blessed the work of his hands, and his substance is increased in the land. But put forth thy hand now, and touch all that he hath, and he will renounce thee to thy face._ JOB 1:6-11

――――――――――――――――――― ―က― ―――――――――――――――――――

SITUATION: A woman has a male friend with whom she has had a long term friendship and has shared many life experiences with.

When the woman meets a romantic interest, her male friend appears to feel slighted as the woman's attention is being directed towards her new interest and begins to make comments as "he doesn't want to bother her" or "maybe he shouldn't call as often as before" since she is entertaining a new gentleman. The woman still maintains value in her friendship with the man, however she is confused as to why he would react this way, particularly since she had previously made herself available to him as a love interest and he did not respond. Question: Why should the man have any feelings one way or the other about the woman's new love interest when he didn't act when he had ample opportunity?

THOUGHT: The only time we don't like Praise is when it's going to somebody else. Looks like this brother had the opportunity to claim this woman as his own, however, didn't capitalize on it until it was too late, or he saw that someone else was now interested. You always miss your water when the well runs dry. Why is it always like that??? It's because we're not paying attention to what's right before our very own eyes. What a wonderful thing it is when we do recognize and react on it. The two hearts beating as one is the missing piece to the puzzler; when it's a perfect fit, it feels good, and you know it. I'll say it again the one that recognizes the gift of a woman's heart is the blessed one, and is rewarded greatly. It's never personal; his loss is someone else's gain. He can't be mad at anyone but himself; that's why he sends those lame text messages. Brother you need to get yourself a life 4 REAL and leave this involved woman alone.

How Would You Handle It?

_____

_____

_____

_____

What Does God's Word Say About It?

One thing have I asked of Jehovah, that will I seek after; That I may dwell in the house of Jehovah all the days of my life, To behold the beauty of Jehovah, And to inquire in his temple. PSALM 27:4

—⚒—

SITUATION: What do you do when you have met someone (a man) who is a great catch but their presence and accomplishments intimidate you?

THOUGHT: Don't be intimidated; rather seek to get to know him and what makes him tick. Men really are simple and it doesn't matter how much they have accomplished, they still like or want a down to earth, but supportive woman that will love, respect, soften and enhance them. We were created as women to walk beside, not behind them, to be one in the flesh, and not beneath them. Now if the two of you got it like that and would prefer to walk equally then that's cool too, but never disrespect them while you're there; they love to be appreciated and ego stroked, so keep it coming ladies and you can have the world from them, there isn't nothing they wouldn't do for you. It wouldn't also hurt if you were a "Virtuous Woman" in the process; check her out, she's bad!!! She's priceless, far above rubies; she brings him good and not harm; she is God-fearing; she works with her hands; not like a diva or prima donna; she provides for her husband and family, and she's intelligent and has business sense, which enables her to provide earnings to her family; her home is kept well and she represents her husband in her appearance and around others with respect, finally she speaks wisdom and seeks to build up and not tear down. He who finds her will be blessed in the city and in the fields, blessed coming out and going in.

How Would You Handle It?

_____

_____

_____

_____

What Does God's Word Say About It?

A worthy woman who can find? For her price is far above rubies. The heart of her husband trusteth in her, And he shall have no lack of gain. She doeth him good and not evil All the days of her life. She seeketh wool and flax, And worketh willingly with her hands. She is like the merchant-ships; She bringeth her bread from afar. She riseth also while it is yet night, And giveth food to her household, And their task to her maidens. She considereth a field, and buyeth it; With the fruit of her hands she planteth a vineyard. She girdeth her loins with strength, And maketh strong her arms. She perceiveth that her merchandise is profitable: Her lamp goeth not out by night. She layeth her hands to the distaff, And her hands hold the spindle. She stretcheth out her hand to the poor; Yea, she reacheth forth her hands to the needy. She is not afraid of the snow for her household; For all her household are clothed with scarlet. She maketh for herself carpets of tapestry; Her clothing is fine linen and purple. Her husband is known in the gates, When he sitteth among the elders of the land. She maketh linen garments and selleth them, And delivereth girdles unto the merchant. Strength and dignity are her clothing; And she laugheth at the time to come. She openeth her mouth with wisdom; And the law of kindness is on her tongue. She looketh well to the ways of her household, And eateth not the bread of idleness. Her children rise up, and call her blessed; Her husband also, and he praiseth her, saying: Many daughters have done worthily, But thou excellest them all. Grace is deceitful, and beauty is vain; But a woman that feareth Jehovah, she shall be praised. Give her of the fruit of her hands; And let her works praise her in the gates.

PROVERBS 31:10-31

SITUATION: My desire to counsel and be of assistance to my friends in their times of need and confusion has carried over into my dating life. I have more often than not taken on the role of the therapist to men who have initially approached me as a potential mate, but have left the situation either reconciled with an ex or contemplating other opportunities. Sometimes this is due to the fact that the man may not have been that interested in me all together and that I was simply a convenient sounding board for him to get him to his true destination, however in most instances I am the actual instigator for this behavior. I have an inquisitive mind and will often ask probing questions that will lead the man down a path he may not have intended to go, and thus opening doors of possibilities that he may not have entertained had I not pointed them out.

THOUGHT: This begs the question if I, or any other woman in this situation has the subconscious thought that she may not indeed be worthy of a good relationship. This type of behavior is classic self-sabotage and is a mechanism for driving things away as opposed to bringing us abundance. I doubt there is much coincidence that the very thing you claim to crave is the first thing you tend to find excuses not to have once it's presented. Brothers know from the very beginning if they are interested or not; problem here is they don't know how to let us down easy once they realize there's no love connection between the two. "They always want to save-a-girl for a rainy day"; when they should just be honest enough to say, they only need advice and keep it moving. We are not always the damsel in distress!!! But because we are emotional beings, many times we miss diagnose what's really happening and when we see that he's just not that into us, we try and shift the conversation in another direction, when we really should keep it moving and not expect something in return, that way our feelings won't get hurt in the process. If we listen, a man really will tell us what he wants or needs us to know. Listen up Agnes!!!

How Would You Handle It?

_____

_____

_____

_____

What Does God's Word Say About It?

> _Beloved, believe not every spirit, but prove the spirits, whether they are of God; because many false prophets are gone out into the world._
> I JOHN 4:1

> _But I say unto you, love your enemies, and pray for them that persecute you._ MATTHEW 5:44

———m———

SITUATION: Middle-aged woman, in transition (early days of post-divorce after a later-in-life marriage), childless, feels quite alone in the world as she lays in bed sick, realizing that there's no one on whom to call (no significant other, no immediate family within 200 miles) if she needs anything.

THOUGHT: Lo, I am with you, even until the end of the earth. Being alone, but not lonely isn't a bad thing. Sometimes God will purposely leave us in an alone state, that he may minister to our heart and mind for where he's taking us; our destiny is so important; many times it's that very thing that the enemy tries to robe us of; he tries to defeat us before we get to that place where God can really use us. You need to STOP sometimes and look at the reason you are in the place you're in. Was it by choice or was the decision to be alone decided for you; we either choose to be alone or choose not to be alone. Are you inviting, or welcoming, or do you close everyone out around you or is it because of previous relationships that you are alone. Being alone is a state of mind and not a condition. Choose to open up your heart and mind to receive someone into your space; JUST DO IT!!! Step out on faith and see how different your life will be.

How Would You Handle It?

_____

_____

_____

_____

What Does God's Word Say About It?

> *Teaching them to observe all things whatsoever I commanded you: and lo, I am with you always, even unto the end of the world.* MATTHEW 28:20

> *Yea, thou I walk through the valley of the shadow of death, I will fear no evil; for thou art with me; Thy rod and thy staff, they comfort me.* PSALM 23:4

> *Now faith is assurance of things hoped for, a conviction of things not seen.* HEBREWS 11:1

SITUATION: You and your brother are not on the best of speaking terms, you hadn't seen him in over 8 years due to difficult circumstances; you attend a funeral of a longtime family friend. You know he'll be there so you take the trip in hopes of uniting with him. Upon arriving the 1st person you see is someone who you have kicked it with over the years; he wants to see and spend time with you after the wake. Following the wake, you're still trying to connect with your brother, who doesn't know you made the trip; you desperately try to get his attention and it fails, because you're too far away, but you keep pushing through the crowd and just as you were about to give in and leave with your old flame, you turn around and your brother's back was hands length away from you; The reunion was great; and you actually end up staying with your brother and not your old flame where you would have been tempted to do something you really didn't want to do and especially when the two of you are now both married.

THOUGHT: I really believe that God blesses our efforts; Evil's always present, and when you're in it, you're not really thinking about it; "Oh, I should have not done this sinful act;" You're too caught up in the moment to think anything different; nor do you say, "Oh, this feels so bad." while you're doing it either; that actually comes after the natural act; If we were more conscience of what and why we do certain things then we probably would be more able to walk away from some of the sinful things we get into and feel much better inside and out for it afterwards.

How Would You Handle It?

_____

_____

_____

_____

What Does God's Word Say About It?

There hath no temptation taken you but such as man can bear: but God is faithful, who will not suffer you to be tempted above that ye are able; but will with the temptation make also the way of escape, that ye may be able to endure it. I CORINTHIANS 10:13

—m—

SITUATION: When God says, "When you get sick and tried of being sick and tried, you'll do something about it." I left that marriage and never looked back. Now, was that right or wrong; who's to say?

THOUGHT: You and your spouse knew what went on in that marriage. There are (3) sides to every story; yours, theirs and the actual. You don't owe anyone an explanation as to why you chose to leave other than God himself. If infidelity occurred in the marriage, and you were unable to reconcile, it was the right thing to do; as God gives instruction as to why you should leave, not man. There is life after Divorce; chalk it up as experience; forgive, heal and move on with your life baby.

How Would You Handle It?

_____

_____

_____

_____

What Does God's Word Say About It?

And if she herself shall put away her husband, and marry another, she committeth adultery. MARK 10:12

For the woman that hath a husband is bound by law to the husband while he liveth; but if the husband die, she is discharged from the law of the husband. ROMANS 7:2

—⁓—

SITUATION: I've dated a couple of men in my lifetime; and often wonder what makes one man better than the next???

THOUGHT: Some are better at sex; some more romantic; some are more of a provider than others; some make you feel like you're the only one in the world; some will never cheat; some will. All depends on what you like; need or want. The best way to determine is how he treats or makes you feel in or out of his presence. What's good for one may not be good for the other. If you got a GOOD MAN, you had better let him know it and treat him right, as well; let him know he's appreciated by stroking his ego, cuz if you don't someone else will. We as women should always pray and keep our brothers, husbands and son's lifted up at all times. When a man tells you, "you make him feel like a King," he is well pleased with you; never take him for granted or disrespect him.

How Would You Handle It?

_____

_____

_____

_____

What Does God's Word Say About It?

With all prayer and supplication praying at all seasons in the Spirit, and watching thereunto in all perseverance and supplication for all the saints, EPHESIANS 6:18

—⚬—

SITUATION: Sometimes in life you have to go through all of the bad to get to the good. You really do have to kiss a few frogs before you actually get to your Prince Charming. Why did it take me so long to get to this place; now that I'm here how do I maintain???

THOUGHT: Be true to yourself and the person you're with; love like it's heaven on earth. You have to learn from your past mistakes; most of all God has to break, re-make, re-shape, and mold you for his Glory. Despite the heartaches and disappointments it took to get here, it was all worth the ride, I'm sure. Sometimes you have to know what the bad feels like in order to appreciate the good. Tyler Perry's "Diary of a Mad Black Woman" Is one of my favorite movies; I can recite almost every scene, especially when Kimberly Elise's character, Helen, had to get mad before she could reap the benefits of a good man - "I'm not bitter. I'm mad as hell." she quotes, and then she realizes that Shemar Moore's character, Orlando had to show her what love from a real man was really like, ooh, I get goose bumps just thinking about it:

Helen: [upon seeing Orlando staring at her] What?

Orlando: I'm just sittin' here, tryin' to think of a way to say this to you.

[pauses]

Orlando: I'm in love with you.

Helen: How do you know that?

Orlando: I don't know how to explain it to you.

Helen: Try.

Orlando: Helen, if I'm away from you for more than an hour, I can't stop thinking about you. I carry you in my spirit. I pray for you more than I pray for myself. I've got it so bad for you I'd... I'd go to the grocery store and buy your feminine products, I swear I would.
[Helen and Orlando laugh]

Orlando:	And see? And that... that... That smile. Helen, when you smile like that, my world... It's all right.
	[pauses]
Orlando:	I am in love with you.

How Would You Handle It?

_____

_____

_____

_____

What Does God's Word Say About It?

Love never faileth: but whether there be prophecies, they shall be done away; whether there be tongues, they shall cease; whether there be knowledge, it shall be done away. I CORINTHIANS 13:8

—m—

SITUATION: Why is it that some people only call you when it's necessary for them; I mean when they're in need or when they're going through a test; Then after they're doing better you don't hear from them anymore. This is so disturbing; and when you see them, they look like they have it altogether, and really didn't need your help after all. NOT!!!

THOUGHT: These type of peeps are users, who have never learned to be accountable to anyone other than themselves; they also tend to think it's all about them, however, when they are broke, busted and disguised, they want the whole wide world to know that they're going through, because they really can't do it alone and really do need others to survive; after they've gotten what they need from you, they go back into their self-centered life, like nothing ever happened, like you didn't do anything to assist in bringing them out. The best way to deal with these types of peeps is to acknowledge what they are doing, pray for them and keep it moving, by not investing a lot of your precious time with their dilemmas. In the words of my Pastor, "Take it to Jesus." Intercession is good, but by the time it takes to call another person, you could have already asked God for help yourself. What's that Trinity Hymnal we us to sing in the Old Baptist Chu'ch - "Ask the Savior to help you comfort, strengthen and keep you; He is willing to aid you, He will carry you through." Look ever to Jesus, He will carry you through; Now, that's a WRAP.

How Would You Handle It?

What Does God's Word Say About It?

And all things, whatsoever ye shall ask in prayer, believing, ye shall receive. MATTHEW 21: 22

Confess therefore your sins one to another, and pray one for another, that ye may be healed. The supplication of a righteous man availeth much in its working. JAMES 5:16

SITUATION: If someone ask you to marry them after being involved for three months, would you accept or decline the proposal, only to fine out afterwards that they really wasn't the person for you?

THOUGHT: I know that you never stop learning a person, even after years of marriage, I'm not sure if I would marry a person after three months of dating; I would, however, consider after six months to a year, or even possibly two years. Anything over three years is too long to still just be dating without some idea of where you're going or planning to go with the relationship.....I polled a couple of males who miraculously said the same thing; They said they would at least like to see what a person was like during all four seasons. This brought up a valid point, someone might be a spring/summer, which means they may turn into a whole new person and party and act wild during that season, then revert back to their normal self afterwards, during the fall/winter; You may or may not can handle that behavior. Take your time; get to know the person, it's never good to rush into anything. Even as fine wine has to marinate over a period time; the longer it does the better it is. In the same manner you should let your relationships and marriage run its course as well. The more you learn about the person, the longer you could possible be together, that's if you like what you've learned about them.

How Would You Handle It?

_____

_____

_____

_____

What Does God's Word Say About It?

> *For everything there is a season, and a time for every purpose under heaven: a time to be born, and a time to die; a time to plant, and a time to pluck up that which is planted; a time to kill, and a time to heal; a time to break down, and a time to build up; a time to weep, and a time to laugh; a time to mourn, and a time to dance; a time to cast away stones, and a time to gather stones together; a time to embrace, and a time to refrain from embracing; a time to seek, and a time to lose; a time to keep, and a time to cast away; a time to rend, and a time to sew; a time to keep silence, and a time to speak; a time to love, and a time to hate; a time for war, and a time for peace.* ECCLESIASTES 3:1-8

———————————— ~m~ ————————————

SITUATION: You're a dog lover in a new relationship and a major problem surface that affects the other person's health. The person is asthmatic and has allergies very bad;   while visiting your place they have a major out-break. How do you handle this sensitive issue and save the relationship in the process?

THOUGHT: Early on in a new relationship it's so important to discuss all concerns no matter how large or small, as this will be a determining factor whether you go forward or not in the relationship. Nothing beats understanding and communication. You have to pray, talk and come to a conclusion to be able to resolve any issue that comes your way; and, especially if it concerns someone's health, I mean you really have to put that baby to bed so that you can move on. You don't want to be incentive or too reactive, but you do want to be smart and make the best sound decision conductive to your situation. This is also a way to see how he/she will handle problems in the future. It really is about being an accountable and responsible person in your relationship and to one another.

How Would You Handle It?

_____

_____

_____

_____

What Does God's Word Say About It?

A soft answer turneth away wrath; But a grievous word stirreth up anger. PROVERBS 15:1

Be ye angry, and sin not: let not the sun go down upon your wrath: EPHESIANS 4:26

SITUATION: What is it about women, when they see a brother/man get a house and drive a new car, that he's all of a sudden attractive or more liked??? I'm a man and I don't do that when I see a woman with a nice home or car.....It doesn't make me attracted to her or want to be with her because of what she has. I'm sure a lot of other men agree with me. This may be because we are attracted physically to ya'll and the emotions come later. I don't want anyone to want me for the things I have. Heck, for all they know, I just might be struggling trying to pay for them....LOL having a house and a car, doesn't mean I'm rich or have money. Is this a black female thing or female in general???

THOUGHT: Let me first say that we all like nice things and would like to live as comfortable as possible. This is such a great situation and question for us ladies. Generally speaking you have all types of women out there; some are looking for a good man who will just treat them right and it doesn't really matter what they drive, as long as they have reliable means of transportation, their own place to stay, and not at home with mama and a job. However, there are also the gold-digger's who won't even look at a brotha unless they are driving a new or particular type of car, live in the most prestigious and pricey area and have a job making bank. They have that "show-me-the-money" mentality; that's all their looking for or want, nothing else matters. Sometimes we as women wanna be in a man's life so badly that we miss the substance of the man in the massive cloud of what he has; then realizes that we have nothing outside of his stuff. Scripture says: "For the love of money is the root of all evil", it's not the fact that money is present; it's the love of it. Be careful not to get it twisted!!! Here's a thought, if he lost everything would she still want to be with him??? Inquiring minds do want to know...I once heard a person say that nobody wants to be with a person that no one else doesn't want;

I see it like this, at the end of the day, that's still his car and his house, it doesn't mean that I get it too just because I'm in a relationship with that person. I want to know who the man is outside of all that stuff, what his relationship is with God, and what he really stands for. I like nice things, but I am not the Material Girl that Madonna once sang about. Regarding your question on if it's a black female thing or female in general. I do believe it's a female thing in general. We are all looking for some type of security within the person we chose to be in a relationship with.

How Would You Handle It?

_____

_____

_____

_____

What Does God's Word Say About It?

But Peter said, Silver and gold have I none; but what I have, that give I thee. In the name of Jesus Christ of Nazareth, walk. ACTS 3:6

For the love of money is a root of all kinds of evil: which some reaching after have been led astray from the faith, and have pierced themselves through with many sorrows. I TIMOTHY 6:10

—ω—

SITUATION: Recently a friend started dating a really nice and eligible guy who really pursued and courted her the right way. They talked daily, had weekly dates where they spent time sharing intimate moments with one another, and he even begin expressing his true feelings as in love for her, but 6 months into the relationship he begin to be distant and finally told her that he had a problem with commitment and was going to have to break the relationship off, but still wanted to call and talk to her over the phone like nothing had ever happened; you talking about a real heartbreak for my friend because no one had ever treated her the way this man had, by expressing his true feelings thru romantic dates and sharing, she begin to fall in love with the illusion of this man only to have the bomb dropped that he wasn't ready or capable of committing 6 months later, and he was a man after God's own heart.

THOUGHT: Why, I'm, At Pause…..Sounds like one of those Lifetime Movie Stories; you know where the man comes into the woman's life showing her with love and affection only to find out that he's not who he says he is or is living a double life. You could also call is "Theft through Deception", because that's what happens he gave her a false security of something that he wasn't capable of delivering. He deceived her by advertising something that he was FRESH out of, with no intention of an IOU or Rain check. T.D. Jakes says it like this; "there's nothing worth advertising something that you are out of." If you know that you don't have the capacity to love, then stop advertising that you are a loveable person; and if you know that you are not prepared to make a commitment to another person, then stop advertising that you want to be in a exclusive committed relationship, I mean all over the dating and social-networking sites advertising that you are single and available and looking for commitment, when you are fresh out of it. Not you, but your neighbor; again, you know how you chu'ch folk do it. I say "chu'ch" folk, because I'm sure, that Christians aren't going around making false advertisements of themselves; but the sad thing is this is the game that people are playing in today's society as well as in church. Can you say playing games, with a capital "G" Perpetrating with no return on an investment; even to the point that you no longer pick up the phone to call a relationship off, as it's now done via text message. Did the person ever mean anything to you, if so; you should at least have more respect for them than breaking up via text. IJS

How Would You Handle It?

_____

_____

_____

_____

What Does God's Word Say About It? ?

> *Thy tongue deviseth very wickedness, Like a sharp razor, working deceitfully.* PSALM 52:2

> *Lying lips are an abomination to Jehovah; But they that deal truly are his delight.* PROVERBS 12:22

SITUATION: You receive a casual text from an ex-lover asking you to have an affair with him on the side, problem here, you both are seeing other people. You advise this person that you are in an exclusive and committed relationship and you're perfectly happy where you are, and don't accept his offer. You admit that when the two of you were together, you were also committed to being in that relationship with him, and wouldn't expect to do anything less with the person you're currently involved with. When you turn him down, he tells you that you can have an affair with him, as you're not married to this person; and it should be find for the two of you to spend quality time together. After all he's not asking you to leave the other person; he's only asking you to have an affair with him. WOW!!!

THOUGHT: What a selfish and inconsiderate gesture!!!! My fist remark to this situation was, "Is this person CraZy, or just playing like it." Did he not hear you say, that you were in an "exclusive committed relationship, and that you were happy there?" guess that didn't mean anything to him, or the fact, that he's also in a relationship with someone else. See that's the problem today, people aren't serious about the relationships their in…they just play around with one another's feelings like it's nothing. I'm sure his friend wouldn't feel the same way if she knew he was out soliciting himself like that. And I did refer to it as soliciting, because that's what he's doing asking another woman to agree to have an affair with him, knowing that they are both in relationships with other people. I'm really Grieved at his behavior, and hope this sister, stands firm in what she believes and not entertain this person's cravings at all. Sounds like he has that mentality of David for Bathsheba, an appetite or craving for something that by law he couldn't have but wanted so badly that he lied and betrayed to be with her. You know the story - "David lies with Bathsheba, and she conceives - He then arranges for the death in battle of her husband, Uriah." Now, you see that lead to the death of another, and unhealthy and unsafe circumstances for him in the end. What might start off as innocence, always leads to lying, deceitfulness and covering up only to justify your own selfish behavior; when you count up the cost, it's never worth it. Sin truly does affect everyone involved.

How Would You Handle It?

_____

_____

_____

_____

What Does God's Word Say About It?

> *Bread of falsehood is sweet to a man; But afterwards his mouth shall be filled with gravel.* PROVERBS 20:17

> *Take heed lest there shall be any one that maketh spoil of you through his philosophy and vain deceit, after the tradition of men, after the rudiments of the world, and not after Christ.* COLOSSIANS 2:8

> *And I will cause them to eat the flesh of their sons and the flesh of their daughters; and they shall eat every one the flesh of his friend, in the siege and in the distress, wherewith their enemies,* JEREMIAH 19-9

Part V

"You will not surely die, said the Serpent to Eve. . ."

No Apologies, No Excuses

CHU'CH - RELIGION - FORBIDDEN THINGS

SITUATION: There is a person who loves God; constantly seeks a close intimate relationship with God; and wants to please God in all they do. That person has done all they know to do to surrender themselves up to God and allow Him to take the lead in their life. After much prayer and confirmation, that person believes in their spirit that God has revealed a certain plan and purpose for their life. The person prays for open doors and guidance as they begin to walk and as they walk in the path of that certain plan and purpose. Although their spirit tells them, this is what God is calling them to and although doors are opening, there is a constant, overwhelming struggle that makes the person feel alone, feel hurt, feel discouraged and feel like giving up because it seems like they will never find stability, peace and a sense of accomplishing God's plan and purpose. How does that person find the strength and motivation to stay the course and refuse to give up???

THOUGHT: The enemy always wants to rob, steal and kill; actually it's his job and purpose in life to confuse and keep you wondering about what God wants you to do, if it's right, his purpose or plan. If God has provided confirmation, then what are you waiting for??? The one thing that I love about God during this time is that he never allows his plan and purpose for your life to leave your mind.....you focus and think about it regularly, and that's how you know that it's from God; because he keeps it on the forefront of your mind daily. It's so close you can taste it, I mean; it's the air you breathe. The only thing left to do is Just Do It; just as picking up that cross and following him daily is a chore, so it picking up your plan and purpose, you simply have to Just Do It; you've searched for answers and God has given you the answers; just as he knew that he had to go and die for our sins, yet, he still ask his Father, "Can this bitter cup pass" knowing that he still had to go forth, he was willing to do it, in obedience to his Father. In that same obedience, you have to Just Do it; I've learned that whatever God calls you to, he's already equipped you for it; know that opposition will always be present; you have to Just Do It. He'll provide whatever else you need; stability, peace, sense of accomplishment, etc. God's got all of that right in the palm of his hands....Whatever you need, God's got it!!! Trust me on this one He's just waiting for you to step out on Faith and Just Do It!!! It's never easy, you make the effort, and he will provide the resources. My final word to you is to Just Do It!!! You'll see how richly blessed your life will be and how quickly it will change. Just Do It!!!

How Would You Handle It?

_____

_____

_____

_____

What Does God's Word Say About It? ?

Now faith is assurance of things hoped for, a conviction of things not seen. HEBREWS 11:1

And he went forward a little, and fell on his face, and prayed, saying, My Father, if it be possible, let this cup pass away from me: nevertheless, not as I will, but as thou wilt. MATTHEW 26:39

SITUATION: Why is it that our worship and activities surrounding worship discontinues or slacks when we get involved in a new relationship, instead of inviting our new found love to come and participate with us; what we tend to do is everything but come to church. We escapade all over the city; seen at plays, restaurants, parties, etc., but not at church; idolizing them like their God's. What's that about???

THOUGHT: This reminds me of that quote from the 1991 Movie "New Jack City", another one of my favorite movies, of which I can quote many lines… "Idolater! Your soul is required in hell!" The primary reason that relationships doesn't work is because we don't invite God in on our decision making process; without him involved it's never going to work successfully; key word here is successfully. Secondly after we are involved and all in love, we show more love and affection for the person and less to the giver of the GIFT. And we already know that the God we serve is a JEALOUS GOD. If he or she's truly sent by God, then they'll want to participate and give back to God for what he's given the two of you, freely. Don't get it twisted, all gifts aren't from God, and we have an odd way of showing our appreciation when we do get a good thing. Like they say, "The family that prays together stays together."

How Would You Handle It?

_____

_____

_____

_____

What Does God's Word Say About It? ?

For I am persuaded, that neither death, nor life, nor angels, nor principalities, nor things present, nor things to come, nor powers, nor height, nor depth, nor any other creature, shall be able to separate us from the love of God, which is in Christ Jesus our Lord.

ROMANS 8:38-39

SITUATION: It's Sunday morning and you're in a leadership role in your church; for whatever reason you decide to wear something that's wasn't appropriate attire for Sunday morning; it was just too tight and too revealing. Someone from the Advisory Board confronts and addresses your attire, as they felt it wasn't appropriate, as it could have caused someone to stumble or become distractive. How do you handle this issue???

THOUGHT: In most cases the common attitude of the church is "come as you are," but come as you are doesn't mean that you come in the 1st thing that you pull out of your drawer or clothes closet; or that the clothes that you desire to wear have to be peeled off of you either; you have to be a little smarter in your judgment/decisions to wear one thing over another. Your attire shouldn't be distracting; offensive or misleading; we don't want a person to miss the word or the intention of the word because they are too busy focusing on what you have on; you never want to stand out in a crowd, especially when you're a greeter, usher, choir member, or in an auxiliary that should be uniformed or seen as one. And it's not to say that anyone's judging either. It's called take-a-second look;

if you have thoughts about what you're wearing before you leave the house, then you probably shouldn't wear it. And if you're married you'll not only representing yourself, but your spouse as well, so it wouldn't be a bad idea to ask your spouse's opinion. You should never let your "glory and honor, dominion and power" be offensive in the manner of how you dress in chu'ch; everybody isn't saved. And you know how we chu'ch folk are; we will look and comment on what we see, not you, but your neighbor. LOL!!!

How Would You Handle It?

_____

_____

_____

_____

What Does God's Word Say About It? ?

> *In like manner, that women adorn themselves in modest apparel, with shamefastness and sobriety; not with braided hair, and gold or pearls or costly raiment;* I TIMOTHY 2:9

———————————— ⁓ɷ⁓ ————————————

SITUATION: All your life you've tried to do the right things to please your family and others; you've hidden your lifestyle from your family and friends long enough, and don't feel the need to continue doing so any longer. Love finally finds you in a place that isn't pleasing to your family and friends; you decide that it's time to come out, and open your heart to a temptation that you've fought for a long time; you embrace that alternative relationship with the likes of another such as yourself. Even though you know it's not pleasing in the sight of God; you go into this new relationship heart first, openly and freely; giving it all you got; it's all new to you, and it feels so right; you finally decide to give love back to a person that loves you unconditionally as well.

THOUGHT: Even though the decision to love another such as yourself is an abomination in the sight of God, I have no room to judge, as that's for God and God alone to chastise. My prayers are that you continue to seek God and allow him to fashion and change your heart or decision in the choices you make, not my place, for I am not he. Deborah Cox probably puts it better than I, "How did you get here nobody's spose to be here; I've tried that love thing for the last time; my heart says no no nobody's spose to be here but you came along and changed my mind." God has to also change or correct that behavior as well.

How Would You Handle It?

_____

_____

_____

_____

What Does God's Word Say About It? ?

> *Judge not, that ye be not judged. For with what judgment ye judge,
> ye shall be judged: and with what measure ye mete, it shall be
> measured unto you. And why beholdest thou the mote that is in thy
> brother's eye, but considerest not the beam that is in thine own eye?
> Or how wilt thou say to thy brother, Let me cast out the mote out
> of thine eye; and lo, the beam is in thine own eye? Thou hypocrite,
> cast out first the beam out of thine own eye; and then shalt thou see
> clearly to cast out the mote out of thy brother's eye.* MATTHEW 7:1-5

---—m—---

SITUATION: As a young woman I remember being told by a special
and influential person in my life that she was going to live a life that
was unpleasing to God; I wondered what could have happened to her
that made her want to spend a part of her life with another such as
herself. Was she unhappy with men; had she been hurt so badly by a
man that she never wanted to be touched or held by one ever again; I
pondered and pondered this for a long time to come; I never got the
chance to really explore this issue with her before her death, but was
assured by her that she did live the best life, and that she experienced
everything she wanted to in this life and gracefully went on to be
with her maker; free and forgiven of all the sins she had ever done.
Maybe it was just a phase, as she did eventually go back to having a
relationship with a man, who she loved and who loved her until the
day she died.

THOUGHT: He is, He is, He is…Man looks at the outward; but God looks at the heart; He alone is worthy to judge; he alone is able to discipline; He alone is able to make a wrong a right; He alone brings light and not darkness to a mean and perverted world; He causes the sun to shine and the rain to fall; He is the first and the last; He is the beginning and the end; He makes all things possible; He alone calms the raging seas; He is God Alone, He is God Alone; He really is all that and a BIG bag of your favorite chips!!! Tell someone you know who has experienced, lived, or is living a life not so pleasing to God and shameful in the eyes of man, I "FU" which means I Forgive U; in the words of Cee Lo Green. They need to know that you love them in spite of the choices they make.

How Would You Handle It?

_____

_____

_____

_____

What Does God's Word Say About It? ?

> If we confess our sins, he is faithful and righteous to forgive us our sins, and to cleanse us from all unrighteousness. I JOHN 1:9

> If my people, who are called by my name, shall humble themselves, and pray, and seek my face, and turn from their wicked ways; then will I hear from heaven, and will forgive their sin, and will heal their land. II CHRONICLES 7:14

SITUATION: You complete a project for a female manager at work, in conversation the two of you discuss foods that you like; she's from India, and as a way of showing her appreciation she invites you over to her house for dinner with other co-workers for Indian Cuisine. You are aware that she's gay, and after arriving realizes that she not only invited co-workers but some of her gay friends over as well. One of her gay friends makes a pass, which puts you in an awkward position. You address the issue by advising the friend that you're not gay, and not interested in her advances, but she continues making passes at you; you advise the manager that you're going to leave before dinner is ready and explained the reason why. The manager immediately addresses the issue with her friend, but you still don't feel comfortable and leaves immediately following dinner because the friend keeps trying to engage you in conversation.

THOUGHT: Let it go Poopalicious, can't you see she's not interested in you or your advances. One can't stop what another person does, but you can put one in his/her place when they have stepped out of line such as this person did. If you like it, I love it, just don't try and force another person to agree with or live a lifestyle which is not conductive to theirs and when the person says no, NO STILL MEANS NO!!!

How Would You Handle It?

_____

_____

_____

_____

What Does God's Word Say About It? ?

*Thou shalt not lie with mankind, as with womankind: it is
abomination* LEVITICUS 18:22.

*For this cause God gave them up unto vile passions: for their
women changed the natural use into that which is against nature:
and likewise also the men, leaving the natural use of the woman,
burned in their lust one toward another, men with men working
unseemliness, and receiving in themselves that recompense of their
error which was due. And even as they refused to have God in their
knowledge, God gave them up unto a reprobate mind, to do those
things which are not fitting* ROMANS 1:26-28

TEST - TESTIMONIES

SITUATION: Sometime ago while going through a rough period in your
life you do something that was bad to another person; something that
could have cost your freedom; was even questioned by the authorities,
but was never charged for this incident, and when finally questioned by
the person that you had wronged, their remarks were; why did you do it;
then advised that it really didn't matter as long as you just fix it, they'd be
alright. When you shared this information with your soon to be husband
at the time; his remarks were; "God likes you" He tells you that if you
didn't think that God wouldn't do what he said he would do, then just
ask Him; you do and God didn't only fix it between you and the person
you had wronged, but he also provided the financial resources for you to
make restitution for your wrong. Now Ain't God Good!!!

THOUGHT: Let's hear it for God!!!! For he will do just what he says he'd do.....He's not a man that he should lie, nor the son of man that he should repent. He loves us for real, and will forgive and forget that sin. There's nobody like him; nobody greater than him, NOBODY!!! You can search long, and you can search wide, but you'll never find anybody that will do what God does, no not one. God's promises are true; when the favor of God is upon you, you will prevail.

How Would You Handle It?

_____

_____

_____

_____

What Does God's Word Say About It? ?

> *God is not a man, that he should lie, Neither the son of man, that he should repent: Hath he said, and will he not do it? Or hath he spoken, and will he not make it good?* NUMBERS 23:19

> *He will again have compassion upon us; he will tread our iniquities under foot; and thou wilt cast all their sins into the depths of the sea.* MICAH 7:19

SITUATION: After being laid-off for over four months, I was hired for a temporary job with a company that I had worked for in the past. It was a blessing in disguised. My Director did all that he could to keep money in my pocket, I mean it was like I was getting $.50 to a $1.00 or more each pay check. One particular morning my Manager came to tell me that she and my Director wanted to see me after lunch; I couldn't imagine what they wanted to see me about, but went on working and just before lunch, I had an urge to go to the copy room; just as I entered, there was a fax immediately coming over which said "the $3K dollar staying bonus that you requested had been approved." This fax was from our Corporate Office which had my name on it. I tell you, I liked to tore that room up shouting and giving praises to GOD, I was whoa; for just months earlier I prayed and asked God for a blessing, not $2K, but $3K and he gave me exactly what I asked for.

THOUGHT: We have not because we ask not. You have to be specific in your request to God. The Caravans use to sing a song back in the days that went a little something like this: "You can't beat God's giving, no matter how you try. And just as sure as you are living and the Lord is in heaven on high. The more you give, the more He gives to you, but keep on giving because it's really true that you can't beat God's giving, no matter how you try." One thing about God, he never sends somebody else to do what he wants you to know he did. He will use someone as the vessel, but he wants you to know for certain that he provided the way for the blessing. God closes doors no man can open & opens doors no man can close. You really have to Ask, Seek and Knock.

How Would You Handle It?

_____

_____

_____

_____

What Does God's Word Say About It? ?

> *Ask, and it shall be given you; seek, and ye shall find; knock, and it shall be opened unto you:* MATTHEW 7:7

WORKPLACE - SEXUAL HARRASSMENT

SITUATION: Worked for a company for six months that insisted on calling me a "1099" or "contract" employee. This provides them with the benefit of paying a straight hourly amount and allowed them to shift the payroll tax liability to the employee. (Federal, state, medicare, work comp, and yes...unemployment as well as benefits...insurance and PTO). My compensation for this opportunity was $2 per hour over my agency pay. After a short time, I requested a meeting to discuss my uncomfortable situation of being called a "1099" employee since I did not feel that according to IRS guidelines my duties and responsibilities were no different than their other employees. The IRS definition of an employee is very narrow. I continued to work for them as they alluded to a promise that they were definitely going to hire me. "Shame on me." But, they decided to eliminate my position due to lack of work after 6 months.

Now, 6 months later...and numerous phone calls to obtain the "1099" that was promised in order to file my taxes, I still do not have such form!!! I just filed for a six-month extension on my income taxes. My next step may be to contact the IRS who will contact them for the form. Or, I could file for unemployment which would open up "Pandora's Box" for them since they would definitely penalize them for not paying me correctly.

THOUGHT: Right is right, and if an individual has provided you a service, you do right to provide until them what's due them, fair and square. Never ever burn bridges, as you never know when you'll need a person or that person will need you again. Deception is never a good principal; and the golden rule still applies today; "do unto others as you would have them do unto you." It cost under a dollar to place a stamp on an envelope today, so what's the big deal; ya'll need to process that "1099" and put it in the mail so this person can take care of her responsibility to the "Modern Day Caesar - Render unto Caesar, what is due Caesar."

How Would You Handle It?

_____

_____

_____

_____

What Does God's Word Say About It? ?

Therefore he that resisteth the power, withstandeth the ordinance of God: and they that withstand shall receive to themselves judgment.
ROMANS 13:2

Render to all their dues: tribute to whom tribute is due; custom to whom custom; fear to whom fear; honor to whom honor. ROMANS 13:7

———————————————— —ɯ— ————————————————

SITUATION: Your immediate boss discovers that you've been out a couple of days due to some medical concerns and text you at home after 9:00 p.m. to see how you're doing. She advises that everybody misses you in the office and that she hopes that you return soon and to take care. It's not un-normal for her to text or call you, but the time of night that she chose to do so on this occasion wasn't normal; not to mention that the next time you were in her office discussing some work related issues, she made an inappropriate gesture with her clothing that was out of character; you have also caught her looking at you inappropriately on a few other occasions. Her daughter is on the debate team, so she reaches out to you regularly to discuss her, then shares confidential office politics with you as well from time-to-time. You respect her personally and professionally and don't want to cross the line, but you can already see where this is heading.

THOUGHT: Keep your conversations with her above the table and very professional. If she offends you, tell her to stop, and report her behavior if necessary. Not crossing the line would be the best thing; dating or having extramarital relationships at work is a no, no, I mean really if this woman's having martial problems or needs to be stimulated she needs to seek counseling or communicate with her husband better, and not be using you for her sexual thrills. Many have tried, but few have succeeded at having a safe and healthy relationship with their bosses at work. Maybe she won't take the offense if you refer her to the EAP; Employee Assistance Program at your company. Sexually Harassment is still alive and well in the workplace; she could use it to turn on you if you get involved and don't like playing her games any longer. Everybody loses. Better safe than sorry.

How Would You Handle It?

_____

_____

_____

_____

What Does God's Word Say About It? ?

> *Put to death therefore your members which are upon the earth: fornication, uncleanness, passion, evil desire, and covetousness, which is idolatry.* COLOSSIANS 3:5

> *But, because of fornications, let each man have his own wife, and let each woman have her own husband.* I CORINTHIANS 7:2

———————————————— —ɯ— ————————————————

SITUATION: You've just been given a new assignment at work, where you've provided info about a new project and attended planning meetings where you offered suggestions. Four months into the project you begin to feel tension and stress from the management team. You don't quite know where this behavior is coming from. You feel almost like you have done something wrong, and could possibly lose your job. Management makes a decision that they know is wrong, and then justifies their reasoning's to favor what you're already doing, then doesn't give you the specific job, instead they put someone else in the role with less experience, and most likely pays them more, and this person still comes to you for answers regarding the position.

THOUGHT: Don't PATRONIZE the person, by having them train the whole entire office, but not allow them to do the job, and then not tell them why the change in behavior. Your prayer daily should be to reverence God for the job; ask that he continues to equip you with the knowledge, skills and abilities to do the job, and most importantly, continue to see him and not the people. What God brings you to he also prepares for you to be there. One thing about knowledge, it's powerful, and no one can ever take away what you know; even though they hate you for it. He says he'll make your enemies your footstool. Relax and watch God work his miracles in your life and even in that job. Sometimes people, like the enemy wants to rob you from where God's taking you, and that'll never happen. GOD is REALLY IN CONTROL and his Favor isn't fair to those who don't understand it. No need to brag or boast, just continue doing what God has called you to do, and he'll take care of the rest.

How Would You Handle It?

What Does God's Word Say About It? ?

Bless them that persecute you; bless, and curse not. ROMANS 12:14

The Lord is my shepherd; I shall not want. He maketh me to lie down in green pastures; He leadeth me beside still waters. He restoreth my soul: He guideth me in the paths of righteousness for his name's sake. Yea, thou I walk through the valley of the shadow of death, I will fear no evil; for thou art with me; Thy rod and thy staff, they comfort me. Thou preparest a table before me in the presence of mine enemies: Thou hast anointed my head with oil; My cup runneth over. Surely goodness and lovingkindness shall follow me all the days of my life; And I shall dwell in the house of Jehovah for ever.
PSALM 23:1-6

Chapter Five

Relationship Tool Box

In Preparation for Marriage

To have a safe and long-lasting relationship

depends on you. Here are some tools that may help

before and after you say "I DO"

I believe in the same thing it took to get a person is the same thing that it needs to take to keep them. Too often in relationships we get to comfortable with our mates and don't think that we need to continue encouraging; loving, dating and expressing our need for them. We don't spend time getting to know them well enough before we go head first into a serious relationship. We don't check the forecast of the relationship enough and before we know it we find our relationships at partly cloudy, windy, scattered thunderstorms or flash floods.

Questions like is this person still my best friend; do I still really like this person; do I still want to spend the rest of my life with them or I'm I just going through a phase for the moment? People come into our lives for a season, a reason or for a lifetime. Which brings me to my main point; I believe that couples who are serious about their commitments to one another should seek counseling before marriage as well as pull and study the marriage vows for a greater understanding of what it says and means to them. Your wedding date is one of the most important days of your lives; many times you are so caught up by the pretty things that you really don't give any thought to what the vows or the preacher is saying. Marriage is the second greatest relationship outside your relationship with God which is the 1st. Here's the equation, **God + Man + Woman = One.**

The word says that the two become one flesh. "And the man said, This is now bone of my bones, and flesh of my flesh: she shall be called Woman, because she was taken out of Man. Therefore shall a man leave his father and his mother, and shall cleave unto his wife: and they shall be one flesh." Look at it as if you're marrying yourself. Each of you should have like interest, goals and love for one another. You should anticipate one another's calls, touch, and idiosyncrasies. And if you find yourself drifting away, you should do whatever it takes to find a way back, if that's truly where you desire to be. Say what you mean, and mean what you say; stop being caught up in the moment, instead try living the life you really want; and let it be an example to others. Try keeping that Sparkle in his or her eyes for a lifetime. Take on that, "Divorce is not an OPTION" attitude and live like you don't have a choice in the matter. I recently saw this on a friend's Facebook post, and immediately sent them my congratulations for hanging in there:

"11 years ago my lover & partner in crime and I were convicted of love in the 1st degree. We stood before God and many witnesses and pleaded "I DO" to those charges brought against us. After hearing our plea, the Pastor sentenced us to "LIFE" in Holy Matrimony. "Marriage was the case they gave us" and we are still guilty and in love!!!!!"

– YOLANDA CLEVELAND-SANDERS

Goes to show you, there is still hope for the hopeless and with love for one another and with God on your side, anything is possible. If marriage is what you want, you have got to commit to staying in it and making it work. It's always easier to throw in the towel and just walk away. Take a few minutes to review the "Marriage Vows" listed below and concentrate on what it says, and then make a mental note of how you felt once you are done. I would even request that you journal your thoughts after reading them for future reference. You'll be surprised how you respond after reviewing these vows and hopefully it will determine if you're ready or not ready to make a commitment of this magnitude. As I'm finding out more and more everyday that individuals are entering into relationships and finding out 6 months or earlier that they are no more ready to be in a committed relationship than the man in the moon, so you know marriage would definitely be out of the question. Which brings me to this conclusion, why not just be honest enough with yourself and the person and let them know early on that you are unable to commit at this time, it would lessen the disappointments for both parties later on, preventing anyone from getting hurt in the process. It's so important to deal with those issues before you take that very important step. Accepting the fact that you are not ready for a relationship is not a bad thing, it's actually the best thing for all involved

"THE MARRIAGE VOWS"

"Dearly beloved, we are gathered together here in the sight of God, and in the face of this congregation, to join together this Man and this Woman in holy matrimony."

"[**Groom's name**], do you take [Bride's Name] to be your wedded wife to live together in marriage? Do you promise to love, comfort, honor and keep her for better or worse, for richer or poorer, in sickness and in health, and forsaking all others, be faithful only to her so long as you both shall live?" Groom: "I do."

"[**Wife's name**], do you take [Groom's Name] to be your wedded husband to live together in marriage? Do you promise to love, comfort, honor and keep him for better or worse, for richer or poorer, in sickness and in health, and forsaking all others, be faithful only to her so long as you both shall live?" Bride: "I do."

By the power investing in him/her then: "I now pronounce you husband and wife.

Chapter Six

Whatcha' Lookin' 4"

What are we really looking for in relationships

before and after we say

"I DO?"

"Whatcha looking for, I'm the one you're lookin' 4
What ya searchin' for, You don't have to search no more
Give you peace and joy, Fill your life with happiness
Don't you look no more, Cause I'm the one your lookin' 4"

LYRICS BY KIRK FRANKLIN

The question was asked and here are the results of what people are really looking for before and after they say that magic word or make that commitment.

You want to marry someone who doesn't want to break God's heart; therefore he/she won't break your heart	You want to marry someone who has experienced something in life; who has had a test, and will openly share their testimonies with you
You want to marry someone who's real with themselves, and knows who they are	You want to marry someone who isn't afraid of communicating or commitment
You want a marriage that is filled with honesty, trust, respect and love that is as unconditional as you can get and you want to have fun doing it	You want to have common interest and goals, and you want to know that your needs will be met
Honesty	Someone who loves for real, for that conquers all
Real true love and honesty from someone who knows and understands that relationships takes work and doesn't mind putting in the time to make it work	Seeking someone who listens, loves and laughs, and who would be able to supplement whatever is needed at the time to make the marriage work
You want to marry someone who first wants to be in a relationship and not just the thought of one	Someone who's not only present, but they must also be emotionally supportive, not allowing issues to keep them from being active in the relationship, as problems will come, but you don't let them over take you, you work through them together
Seeking someone you can get alone with when it really matters	You should find out what your deal breakers are
Who has forgiven and moved forward in life and in relationships	Seeking someone who's not afraid of commitment, and doesn't cop out at the first sign of trouble. Who demonstrates what they've advertised

Chapter Seven

Honesty Test
Would Your Marry Yourself?

HONESTY TEST

Would You Marrry Yourself

Here's what the ladies/gents had to say…

YES	NO	GENDER
I would marry myself b/c I do feel that I have some great qualities which would make a cool partner (i.e. God fearing woman, a sincere interest to commit to a marriage, patience, understanding, positive outlook on life, etc.) However, I honestly feel that I really don't know if I would make a good partner until I am in that situation.	No, I wouldn't marry myself because: I'm too needy; I'm a perfectionist; cares too much about the world, which takes always from my family; I'm not a black or white person; unpredictable; seeks stability. My husband and I balance out one another because we are opposite. In business we work well together; he taught me how to be strong and forceful; I was too wimpy with my family at first, and he taught me to stand up to them. I learned how to trust him without an explanation for everything. I trust that he's going to make the best decision for our family. I can't sleep with the enemy. I remember a time when I would sleep with my face to his, b/c of trust issues, that's not the problem now; I sleep with my back to his now, legs on one another, etc	Female
Yes, I would marry myself or someone like me; double the likeness, and double the fun. Would have a lot in common, same interests, same sense of humor. Feels the world has become too capitalistic, anything goes; focus too much on money and labels; this generation doesn't understand nor practice the vows, no respect for God in their lives and relationships, especially when dating sites openly condones those who are having affairs online; that's not of God. Recommended counseling before marriage and also feels that individuals today are more infatuated in relationships than they are in love with the persons of interest.		Male
Yes, and would be looking for the same.	No, because I have unresolved issues and would not want to put that on someone for a lifetime. I would date myself, but I would not marry myself at this very moment.	Female

Yes/No – Due to unfinished debt. Was married before, pros/cons based on the word; I understand marriage, but didn't apply myself. Man is the head; this was discussed, but didn't decide on the best decisions for the two of us.		Female
I possess qualities that a spouse needs. Just to name a few, submissive, whole, listener, sensitive, communicator and most important of all have a relationship with God		Female
Yes, I would because I know I am a good person. (It has taken me almost 30yrs to realize this!) I know I am NOT PERFECT, but I truly care about people, have good values and morals and those are qualities that genuine people look for in a mate. I respect myself and have respect for other people.		Female
I would marry myself because I am a strong partner and loyal to my lover. I am a great listener and would be my partner's best friend.		Female
Yes, I would - I am first a good friend, and listener and would make a good companion, I bring favor from God. I stand in the gap and pray for God's leadership for my family. I am resourceful, fertile and sexy.		Female
Of course. I try to treat people how I want to be treated.		Male
Yes, because I'm a good person and I have the qualities that most women want or desire.		Male

Yes. Overall, I am a good person. Everyone has their faults. I'm told my biggest is how I say things.		Male
	Interesting question, I would not have three years ago. I was bound by pride and confusion. There was no balance in my life and I did not care about what was important to me. What I know now is that I have embraced the Spirit of Christ and believe in the Holy Ghost power to direct my every path. I am not perfect but I trust the spirit more so than ever before.	Male
I don't know how to answer this. At times, yes and at other times no. Nobody's perfect. I think the bigger question each person has to answer is can you live with the not so perfect parts.		Male
Yes, because I would get to know my inner self, personality, attitudes and knowing what I will and will not accept of myself.		Male
Yes, I would marry myself. It was always important to me growing up that I become a good husband to my wife and a good father to my children. Because it was important to me, I like to think that I make a good spouse.		Male
I would have to say yes, I would marry myself. I think when you're looking for a life partner, you're looking for somebody you can spend the rest of your life with, and I definitely see myself able to spend the rest of my life with myself (haha)		Male

Yes, I'm not perfect, but I try to be the best husband I can be.	Absolutely not; nor would my wife marry herself. My wife and I share similarities but we are opposites in many things. I believe we share the same values and only slightly differ in child rearing. We do get a kick out of not being able to finish a sentence and having the other complete the thought notwithstanding that the topic was out of the blue.	Female/Male
Actually with my outgoing personality and sense of humor for starters, Yes....I would be "love at first sight!" Because I enjoy smiling, laughing, and enjoying how life has its own flow. When people look or observe me they see a man who strives to be motivated and upbeat at all times. I enjoy the "intimacy factor" which is part of relating to me that I do enjoy and desire in life very much. I'm "family oriented" which of course is the second most foundation to having in life with God being first and foremost in all of our lives. I'm a lot of fun to be with, love being spontaneous letting life have it's' way. If marrying me only takes a small amount of time, effort, consistency, and commitment......... then I'm a great catch for myself.		Male
I would marry myself because I am a very confident, handsome, intelligent, secure, family oriented, laid back, honest, loving, caring, open minded, giving, God fearing man with a job and a vision!		Male
	No. Though I have come to realize that a man is worth more than a "paycheck" in a marriage/ relationship, I am not where I would like to be financially to take on a spouse.	Male
Without A doubt...cause if I won't, how can I expect someone to want to marry me?		Male

Chapter Eight

From A Man's
Point of View

—m—

It is important to know

what his point of view is.
If we listen we might learn something.

"From A Man's Point of View"

Here's what they have to say

What are you looking for in a mate or in a relationship?

- I'm looking for a best friend in my mate. In my relationship I'm looking for someone who has the same likes and dislikes as I do.

- Companion, trust, love, attraction, etc.

- Someone that is true to themselves. They can't be true to me if they're not true to themselves first. I like a REAL person. Someone that fears God but also has a relationship with HIM. I can work with the rest of her being.

- Honesty, compassion, integrity and good steward.

- First, someone who loves God. Secondly, a nurturer, gentle as a lamb and firm as a tigress when necessary. Someone who can communicate without being condescending in their approach. I do not believe men or women need to manipulate their mates into doing anything for them. I believe that any and everything that I do for my queen is something I want and will do for her because I simply love her. Thirdly, Trust is very important. I have to be able to trust without looking over my shoulder and neither should she be insecure that she needs to do the same. Lastly, a lover that is a friend.

- I looked for someone who had similar interests and morals as I did. Someone I enjoyed spending time with and would fit in with my family.

- This question is an everyday question that is asked "at will" when two people are in the "getting to know" process. I always come up with the top or "final four". Peace, love, joy, and happiness. Peace, when the two of us can sit down together and enjoy a nice intellectual conversation, talking about anything and everything that flows, no arguments that will stir up emotions, no disagreements that will kill the moment, just a nice time sharing with each other's thoughts on what we have a vision to see for the future in our lives. Love, striving to coming together as "one", showing each other how much we really care about one another in that we would do anything for each other, building that foundation that has the potential to grow and prosper. This takes time to grow but if we are sincere about what we say and what we do everything will come together for the good. Joy, who doesn't want a joyous relationship these days? Who doesn't want to walk around with their mate, their significant other, feeling so secured about being with and around the one you love? What joy it is after waking up thanking God to seeing another day, thinking about the one you are so in love with, can't wait to call him/her in the morning to say, "Good Morning _____!" walking around with a big ol'e grin and smile on the face! Joy is being acknowledged and joy is being seen. Happiness.... wow, who doesn't want happiness in their lives? You're happy when you know you have someone who is in and a part of your life. Happiness comes when you can walk around and she is thinking about you and you thinking about her, and when that phone rings and you see his/her name on the caller ID and you hear

that voice that just makes you grin and smile a mile........
That's part of happiness.

• A Godly woman, a woman who has integrity and one who does not have low self-esteem. She has to be self-motivated, loving, kind, gentle, and has a good sense of humor. She has to also be unselfish.

• I don't have to look anymore because I have everything I ever wanted. I have been happily married for nine months.

• I was looking for someone who was thoughtful and treated everyone the right way. It was important to me that the person I married understood that we are all a part of God's family. It was important to me that the person I married realized that we have a responsibility to take care of others who are less fortunate than us because they are our brothers and sisters.

• What I want in a relationship is somebody who can be by my side during good and bad times. Somebody I can both teach and learn from. Somebody I can grow and become a better person with. I look for the same type of things that I try to exhibit in myself. Honesty, caring, fun, everything positive.

• Having been married for 16 years, we are going to continue to promote being a couple and a family that is built on respect and tolerance.

• I was looking for someone genuinely REAL! Someone who was very confident, secure within themselves, nurturing, loving, honest, doesn't need validation. Someone who is sexy full time and not part time. Someone who knows what it takes to make anything worth having work. Unselfish, motivated and simply down for me no matter what and can get my back through whatever!

- (II Corinthians 6:14) Scripture tells us to not be unequally yoked with unbelievers so, first and foremost, I'm looking for... Someone with whom I am spiritually connected

- Someone who shares similar mindsets (ideologies, viewpoints, etc.)

- someone who shares similar ethical/moral practices

- someone who understands (spiritual) responsibilities and deploys them

- Personal relationship with Jesus that is visible. Good relationship with parents/siblings, if still living. Cleanliness. Good sense of humor. Good money management. Health conscientious. Romantic.

Would you marry someone after 3 - 6 months of meeting them? Yes or no and why?

- Not at all. Marriage may have been discussed but not planned or engaged in 3 to 6 months.

- Probably not. I like to keep relationship's fresh and simple. Once the newness wears off, people lose interest in each other. I feel like people get comfortable with what they have and don't do the things necessary to keep relationships alive. So, I guess what I am trying to say is: People need to get to know one another and make sure that they are in love with someone they can spend the rest of their life with.

- NO, because I really don't know all there is to know about them…. I think 6 months to a year is a good time.

- I was engaged to my wife after 1 year of meeting. We have been married for almost 16 years. We had a connection like no one else I had ever met. She was funny, we liked a lot of the same foods and things and I helped around the house…(LOL)

- No. I believe it takes longer to really get to know someone. My problem with my failed marriage was that I did not take the time to get to know that person. It was trial and error and the error prevailed. Now, is it possible? God can do all things. If it is your actual soul mate, which is sent by God, if you are using your spiritual eye along with your naked eye, you will know who is right for you.

- At this point in my life I would say no. I am a little wiser these days and understand the concept of the "newness factor". I think it takes time to really know someone before making that kind of commitment.

- I know some may think this is a "crazy" question but in actuality it's a legit question and you will get a majority of "No!" than you do of the "yes" but for me I believe in faith and if I step out on it and trust God with my heart and my prayer then I will do whatever and however it takes to create such a radical relationship. Yes, I would do it, and why? Because it would be a decision between two adult people who solely care and love each other and would be responsible for their decisions and their own actions. I have witnessed two…. yes, two couples who got married in 6 months and 8 months respectively. Couples are married, one just had a child, and the other has one in the oven as we speak. It takes open communication, total trust, total honesty, total effort, total commitment, and of course total prayer to making that relations work. Too many of us put time parameters and time constraint on a relationship without giving it the faith to grow and prosper. I've always believed that "what you put into it is what you're bound to get out".

- No, I would need to get to know the person and their personality, their background and family history. Also, I need to see if they have a relationship with God.

- No, I think it takes longer than that to truly get to know someone.

- Yes, I would marry someone after 3 to 6 months of meeting them if it was the right person. There is no sense in waiting if you know it is right.

- No, I would not marry somebody after 3-6 months. That's just not enough time for me to be confident that this is the person I want to spend the rest of my life with.

- You may have an understanding of the person within that time frame but I believe you need a little longer to complete the learning process. Your intention is to maintain married for the remainder of your lives.

- Yes and no. Reason for my answer is because you can be with someone 10 years and still not fully know who they are. And how could anyone know the individual when we are constantly changing and evolving as individuals If the chemistry is there and they do not belong to anyone else then why not? Although you do have to be cautious of the individuals representative.

That's the person presented during those 3-6 months conforming to everything you are looking for in a mate until they get comfortable!

- No. I don't believe that you have really had enough time to ascertain, whether or not, a relationship is marriage worthy in 3-6 months. I do believe that, in that time frame,   you are in a better position to re-evaluate the nature of your involvement and/or relationship to determine if it has that potential.

- No cause that is not long enough for the "getting to know you stage."

Do you really know within 15 minutes of meeting a woman if they are someone you would actually marry? What lets you know?

- Fifteen minutes is not enough time to make that determination. Fifteen minutes may determine if you're physically attracted to the person, but not determine if they are Spouse material.

- No. You have to give relationships time to help you identify what kind of love you have. It may just be infatuation.

- Yes, how they carry themselves. I can tell through conversation or body language…..gotta really observe.   Of course this is looking on the inside….cause if I just left it up to the outside, they would have to have white teeth, long hair(their own), light-skinned, nice breast, nice round butt, nice thighs.

- I don't know if this is true. Actually I was the opposite. After a bad breakup from a previous relationship my wife wanted me to promise her that I would not fall in love with her. I told her that I could not do that and the rest is history.

- I don't believe that. It takes longer to know.

- No. I may know if I wanted to take them out on a date but not walk down the aisle.

- I'm not sure about within 15 minutes but to meet a woman for the first time and when meeting her takes place just meeting her can/will set the tone on whether or not I'm interested in communicating with her. If I meet someone for the first time and as we greet each other and she just happen to greet me with a smile, acknowledging my name, and giving me a hug all at the same time???? Oh my my my.... what a great start that is and if she even sounds excited about seeing and meeting me... IT IS ON!!! The reason why I get excited about this is because a woman knows that she can/will make or break the interest. If she approaches me with all that I have acknowledged then it's a great thing. If she meets me and she seems like she's not really interested by saying "hi", puts her hand out for me to shake introducing herself, and carrying a little attitude with her then "Houston, we got a problem". I know women aren't perfect and can't stay happy at all times but if she seems as if the world owes her everything.... then it's a wrap. Setting the tone for a meeting will create some kind of momentum in the relations.

- It depends on her conversation. If the conversation is positive, and if we are communicating the same ideas; give or take. The key is her positive attitude, seriousness of her body language, and her having eye to eye contact.

- No. I don't think you can know if you would marry someone based on your first impression of them.

- I'm not sure that you can know within 15 minutes if you would marry someone. I do think that you can know in 15 minutes that you wouldn't marry someone.

- No, I do not think that is something I know after 15 minutes. Now, if you change "would" to "could" then I can see myself saying this is somebody I could marry after knowing them for only 15 minutes. But to say I absolutely would, there's just too much you don't know about the other person to say that.

- No, it should take longer than 15 minutes to realize if you are going to marry that person. You may realize in that time frame that you are strongly interested in the person, but certainly not if you share the same values

- It's very possible, but as I stated in the previous question be careful. I will say this though. When you see it you'll know it.

- No. I believe that within that time frame you can get a sense as to whether or not you will invest time in getting to know an individual.

- No...But it lets you know if that is someone you would sleep with.

When in a relationship, how important is it to you to be an active participant in maintaining the union?

- It's very important but at the same time it really takes an effort from both parties. A lop-sided relationship (where one is giving 100% and the other is not) always fails and one of the two parties will get hurt or exhausted and frustrated.

- It very important and both parties have to work together for any relationship to work. I definitely prefer to date someone that has the same/similar goals and objectives.

- Highly important. If I'm not a part, then there is no true relationship. It takes two. The same with God....He can't keep just blessing me and I don't at least bless Him with praise and thank you' s....I have to do my part in the relationship...I gotta study to get to know HIM more...so I can continue to build my relationship with HIM.....guess I should marry God, huh? Waaaaaaan.

- Very important. Marriage is definitely give and take. You have your good months and you're bad. It is a sacrifice for both.

- It is very important that both parties work together to maintain the union. Marriage is work. It is give and take. It is compromise.

- Both sides have to make an effort for things to work.

- I was always taught and told that when you put your best foot forward you can walk "forever" and as long as you continue to walk, walk with faith, walk with confidence, and walk with pride because you are letting everyone by your actions know that you are approaching your goal and/or objective with the best attitude, pride, and confidence ever.

- It is very important to me to start off from the beginning, to show my willingness, to show my drive, and responsibility, and my support for the union of this relationship.

- It is very important to be an active participant in the relationship.

- I hear all the time that marriage is something you have to work at. I guess I'm lucky because my wife and I have a great marriage. We joke about the fact that we don't work at it at all….our love for each other comes naturally. Loving my wife is probably the easiest thing I do.

- I think it is very important to be active in maintaining the union. If you're not an active participant then the union won't last.

- You and your partner must be complete participants in maintaining a relationship. You commit fully in your efforts.

- VERY, VERY IMPORTANT! Even if the other half is not it's imperative that you are doing everything in your power to hold up your end of the bargain as well as holding yourself accountable for your flaws. When things go south at least you know you did your part.

- VERY IMPORTANT!!! All the way back to the beginning of man, we were charged to be cultivators and Jesus.

- Very…What you put in is what you get out.

Would you pursue cultivating your relationship with the same drive/ determination you would use when pursing a personal or professional goal or objective? Why or Why not?

- I would. Just like a personal or professional goal, it is a daily effort to maintain.

- If you don't, you end up wanting different things.

- Not as equally. Because goals and dreams are things that we try to achieve.....A person/love is nothing to be achieved.... it's given/shared....a human being is not a trophy or a certificate. I don't like games....if I have to work extremely hard to get you, then I don't need you like that....either you like me or you don't....NEXT. Now, I will cherish you to the best that I can.....I am a man and we don't always do what the female likes or desire....we are physically driven and not emotionally.

- Yes, if the determination and drive is not there for your marriage it will definitely not work. Both parties have to have the drive. You have to be willing to let the same things go. Women and men are different. What might be important to women may not be to men and vice versa.

- Yes I would use the same drive and determination I would use in pursuing a personal goal in my relationship. It is my desire to have that perfect mate. Is that possible. There is no perfect person without some flaws. However, it is important to communicate as the relationship changes and believe me; they will change because we change. My goals are constantly changing. But, I cannot at this age constantly change mates. I believe that it is important to work at your relationship if it is going to be successful. From my past experience, I believe that rushing into marriage is something that you have to be careful of. I have heard too many people say that if they had an opportunity to remarry the person that they are with, they would not. I may have said the same thing at some point or another. I believe if we take our time in choosing our mates, not based on sex but on developing a life partner, then marriages would be more successful. That is when the better or worse statement has true meaning. When we rush into marriage, we are quick to rush out of it or just be miserable for the rest of your lives where you are wishing or even engaging in extramarital affairs because you love her but you don't like her. Those affairs can be anything from working too much, spending a lot of time at church are at play, and the obvious, adultery.

- You should put forth the same effort but I don't think that's always the case. Sometimes you lose sight of the goal and you need to be reeled back in and refocus.

- Again, I believe what (effort) you put into it is what you get out. Lack of consistency in/of communication shows the lack of interest. Much effort and consistency in communication shows the betterment of the interest. I'm willing to put forth the maximum time and effort to build a foundation of a relationship that has the potential to grow and prosper. If we can come together and give it our all and all.... then the outcome and result could be the blessing of a "lifetime".

- Absolutely. It is in my DNA by the grace of God to pursue His will for me, the same drive that God gave to me in this union.

- I think you can pursue it with the same drive you would use when pursuing other goals because a marriage is just too important to give anything less than your best.

- I definitely put my family above my profession. I never really had dreams of being successful in the work world. I've always wanted to be the best husband and father I can be.

- I think you should put more effort in making sure you and your partner are happy together than you would with your professional goal. Otherwise, what's the point of being with another person if it doesn't mean as much to you. That's why people say family first before anything else.

- Your drive in this relationship should way surpass any career or personal objectives.

- ABSOLUTELY! It's all or nothing!

- I do/would pursue cultivating my relationships with as much determination/ drive as I do personal/professional endeavors (almost to a fault). A healthy relationship is the stimulator that drives me even more to be a better man.

- Even more...Because another person is involved...My goals/objectives only consist of me.

Chapter Nine

The Keys To
A Lasting Courtship and Marriage

THE KEYS TO A LASTING COURTSHIP AND MARRIAGE

By doing these (5) simple things, you are sure to be going in the right direction for making it last. The LONGEVITY of your relationship does really depend on you and your partner agreeing to work through it.

1. Communication - This is vital to a successful relationship; has to be there; can't function fully without it. You need to talk about everything; this isn't the time to keep secrets; deceitfulness is a killer. Getting problems out in the open; discussing your belief system and your future endeavors together is the golden rule; by during this early on in your relationship will help you to maintain and be consistent later on in your relationship.

2. Commitment - To be successful you need to be accountable to one another; agree to be actively present and committed to the relationship and to your partner. You need to work together to build the relationship that each of you want; mean what you said, and do what you mean. It takes 100% on both parts, 50% will never work, and keeps the relationship one sided.

3. Honesty/Trust - Being open is the best way to relate to someone in a relationship; to thine own self be true as well as your partner. For the longevity of your relationship this part will go a long way. I mean, what you have to lose; your partner will respect and love you for it. Never judge one another. It's not about where you are or have been, but definitely about where you're going together that really matters the most.

4. Understanding - Nothing beats it, but it's also important to be calm at the time you are discussing a problem in your relationship. You should never discuss problems when you're angry; look at your issue from all points of views, by doing it this way, makes for a better compromise in the end. In all thy getting, get understanding. Thank God for the word.

5. Team Work - Even though the two becomes one, it still takes two willing participants to make a relationship work; it should be about the we's and not the I's; selfishness never won a game by them selves. Each of you should agree to be a part of every element of your relationship. Make your relationship a project and work on it together; just as you seek to accomplish things at your job, do the same in your relationship; then reward yourself for your achievements to one another. Make it Fun, Interesting and Challenging!!!

Chapter Ten

What It Takes

For a Long-Lasting Relationship

WHAT IT TAKES FOR A LONG-LASTING RELATIONSHIP

As you know we are all different individuals, we come from various cultures, religions and backgrounds, and as we live, we will develop many types of relationships in our lifetime, from important ones, to those that won't matter much at all. I share this with many of the young women that I mentor, that the first example of love or trust that you learn about or see, is from your parents or guardians who affectionately teach us the morals, values and principles that follow us into adulthood. Although they may have short-comings themselves, their still our parents and guardians and what they teach is how we respond, even though it might be different from what was demonstrated. You know how your mama'nem use to say; "do as I say and not as I do." We as women look for our fathers in the men we meet and will ultimately date, and men will sometimes seek a woman who also reminds them of their mothers. That's life and just the way it is. So, I can openly and publicly say that it's all my father's fault that I like tall, dark and handsome men today, because my daddy was all that and a "bag of chips" to me in my young finite world as a child. He would pick me up every Sunday evening for as long as I can remember for my date at Princess Drive-in on Main Street, a burger place in Houston, TX back in the days and would always bring me raisins, because I loved them so much; we would talk about my day, week, etc.....how I was doing in school and many other things. So as you can see I was developing my dating and communicating skills all at the same time, as he was teaching me how I should be treated by a man as well. A man is suppose to provide, protect and lead, at least that what I was taught. Little did I know that would still be embedded in my mind today.

I also loved staying with my grandparents, who also taught me about love, respect, trust, finances, cooking, religion, housekeeping, and just basic responsibilities. I would watch how my grandmother would take special care of my grandfather; his meals would be prepared and on the table for breakfast, lunch, dinner and nightly snacks, daily. The house and laundry was done and clean regularly and the bills were paid on time, they even sat down and discussed what bills needed to be paid together weekly, and most importantly God was always first and our tithe envelopes were prepared before we even got to chu'ch on Sunday mornings. I can recall getting mines for $.50 each week. I learned about oneness and unity from them. She loved him and he loved her. So much so that when my grandmother passed December 1975, two months later my grandfather passed in February 1976; and as I recall their birthdays were even a day apart February 2nd and 3rd, now that's compatibility for you. I wonder if that was the deciding factor for them getting married; could have been, as they were great together, I can't even recall a time that I heard them raise their voices, they had disagreements as in all relationships, but because of God in their lives, I never knew the difference. They were married for 37 years before God called them home. Although a different time and place, they were still willing to work through whatever it took to keep that marriage together. My grandmother was a single mother when my grandfather met her and he married and loved her and my mother as if she was his own. Now, that's love and acceptance all bottled up in one.

Back then they also had time to focus on one another, as they didn't have all the distractions of today, things like the internet, dating sites, Facebook, cell phones etc.....or just living in a city like Atlanta where the ratio of men to women is 100 to 88. WOW!!! Today, we'll divorce a person for any reason. This brings me to the main subject of this section in the book where we'll discuss what it takes for a long-lasting relationship. Nobody teaches you how to be married, so you just have to rely on what examples you have in your lives, or reading self-help books such as this one, finally, you in many instances have to rely on your experiences; which may be good or bad, could be, could be not, who's to say?.....you have to be the judge of that.

Men and women are so different; them being visual, and us emotional. Sometimes men are just not as aware, in tuned or compassionate to the needs of a woman. They sometime also confuse intimacy with sex, and those are simply two different things. Honestly, what I've noticed is it doesn't have anything to do with maliciousness or indifference, they just don't know how to separate the difference between the two. How is it that they can have such an intensive drive and determination when pursuing personal or professional goals or objectives, but not do it with the same tenacity when it relates to taking care of or responding to the needs of their spouses? They just aren't wired that way, but by communicating with your spouse and letting them know what your needs are should aid in you accomplishing a better connection with them and therefore assisting the two of you in getting your needs met fully providing satisfaction to both individuals. First and far most, you want to be in a relationship with someone who equally wants to be in a relationship with you. These things can be accomplished; however, it's going to require some work on both parts. Who better knows how you feel, what you like, or how you like to be touched than you. We as people are not mind readers and we don't have some special devices that notify one of how you really feel, so the only way to determine that is to communicate it to your person. What makes one person feel good could be a total turn-off to another. Taking the time to talk with your spouse and asking those questions would be a good alternative to just going through the motions to then find out that your spouse doesn't like it. Show and tell is good, but knowing what satisfies them is better; playing the guessing game isn't a good idea either. We really don't spend enough time getting to know one another, which is a HUGE problem in relationships; then we wonder why our partners drift off and end up having affairs, etc. Never attack the person, but always address the behavior, by doing so you stop them from shutting down, allowing them to really hear what you have to say. It's not what you say; it's how you say it. I read in an article that when you use "I" instead of "you" relating to a situation, psychologically; it reverses that thing which clears the air and makes for a better conversation between yourself and your mate. It's about responsibility and accountability; "It's elementary, my dear Watson".....it is a valuable tool in building a long-lasting relationship. We are perfectly capable of doing it right, but either don't know how or where to start or just don't want to do it. I've always heard that people do what they really want to do. Anything worth having should be worth working for; the rewards would be simply AWESOME, and you could actually end up having a relationship that could last a lifetime.

It's not always easy to talk about your strengthens and weakness when starting new relationships, but it is important to know what they are so as you get farther into a new relationship you will know what to expect. Your new partner will need to know if you are capable of bringing home the bacon, but not well at distributing it, as in, making enough money, but procrastinates when it comes to paying the bills.

Maybe you don't want or care about the responsibility of paying the bills and would rather your partner be responsible for that task. These are all the things that are important and should be discussed early on. Especially before you get so blinded by the love bug that you can't see anything else that's important or significant to the longevity of your relationship. Just because you are a great accountant, doesn't mean that you want to be the one responsible for that task in your relationship. We'll call this segment Marriage or Relationship 101, and in this session let's think of all the things you need to know when you get married that no one tells you when you first start that new relationship with no prior experience in the area. "Who will be responsible for the finances; where will we live; will my spouse be a stay mom, can we afford it; what's our plan, do we have a plan; do we want to start a family, or does one exist already, if so, where will they attend school." A zillion questions, all basic but they all must be addressed. Hopefully you've at least had some discussion during the dating stage concerning some of these issues, if not, here's what a couple of my friends had to share about things they learned. Take note and be prepared when it's your turn.

Marriage or Relationship 101

You have to forgive, forget, and press forward. Never go to bed angry at one another; if it takes all night, make up and discuss whatever it was to get you angry so you know and understand how to handle it the next time, because there will be a next time.	It's good to have someone to come home too and to share the ups and downs with. Marriage can be good, but challenging you must learn how to communication with one another, as that makes it manageable during those difficult times.	Men after marriage don't get better at courtship because they already got you! You will probably gct 60% less courtship after you tie the knot! So that's when the wife has to take charge and keep the flame going, it's about keeping him interested!

I learned that marriage doesn't change you and it doesn't change him. The same things you were unhappy with about yourself when you were single don't go away after you are married. And the things that bother you about your partner before you were married doesn't instantly seem better just because you got married. Don't hide anything while you're dating, just be yourself. Eventually your secret will come out, which can result in feelings of betrayal, deception or have even worse consequences. It's ok if you don't know exactly who you are when you get married, just be sure your mate accepts you for you and don't expect anything less.	Communication is more than just talking, it is LISTENING!!! I learned that not only is it important to communicate your needs to your partner, it is equally important to LISTEN to their needs as well. I spent 10 years in a marriage to a man that I literally had nothing in common with, but had I paid more attention to what his thoughts and ideas on life were, I would have likely never married him in the first place because they were not evenly yoked with mine.	You cannot change a person into what you want. What you see is what you get and this is something that a woman must understand BEFORE she says I do. Marriage does not magically change people into the type of mate that you want. Pay CLOSE attention to the person they are when they are courting you. They may be a bit more romantic initially, but the bottom line person is always there for you to see. Do not go into a marriage wearing ROSE COLORED GLASSES!
You have to stay connected to GOD no matter what...he is your eyes, your ears to hear and always your first love...whatever you face, you will and are going to run to him for all your needs...God will warn you when things change. That scripture in Proverbs that says he calls for the cunning and skillful woman. Your creative nature will kick in, your seven senses will get sharper, and your wisdom for greatness and your skills to be victorious in all that you can do or become is going to become a breast plate of protection. No matter what comes at you with GOD You will be able to stand.	The importance of recognizing that I don't always have to "win" an argument, or even make my point. Sometimes, it's better to ignore the issue entirely. In essence, I think it's incredibly important to know how to pick the battles. The second lesson I'd share is closely related to the first: learn how to "fight fair." Although it's tempting to lash out at the person with whom we're having a heated discussion, that is far from productive and will only likely plant or sow seeds of resentment. Instead, it really does make a difference if, during those discussions, one makes "I" statements…carefully constructed "I" statements, I might add. Consider the difference between "I hate it when you leave your dirty dishes in the sink" and "I would feel more appreciated and as if you valued my time as much as yours if you would take the time to put your dirty dishes in the dishwasher". Not perfectly constructed examples, but hopefully you get the idea.	I did not know that being married would be as tough as working everyday - adjusting to your spouse's likes, dislikes all the while they are adjusting to yours can become challenging. Also I did not know that people are very sarcastic about married couples - most of what you hear on tv, from friends etc.....is negative. You hardly ever hear of someone's marriage being positive and when you do - someone's always trying to create conflict.

Although relationships are hard and do require a lot of effort, God has equipped us with all the tools we need, we just need to take the time to tap into the resources that already lies within us, and in his word. Experience has been and will always be the best teacher. Like with anything else time and attention to detail is the key; it's all the same. Knowing who you are and what you need or want is the other part of the puzzler. Something as simple as going back to the basis will help you go further in building the best relationship for you. It might not work for anyone else, but if it works for you then that's all that matters. God gave us dominion over everything, so why not use what we got to get what we want for what he created in the first place. "And God blessed them: and God said unto them, Be fruitful, and multiply, and replenish the earth, and subdue it; and have dominion over the fish of the sea, and over the birds of the heavens, and over every living thing that moveth upon the earth," (Gen 1:28). He does all things well. Praise GOD!!! "In the beginning was the Word, and the Word was with God, and the Word was God," (John 1:1). Why reinvent the wheel, when you can use the guidelines already set for you. I'm thankful to be apart of a people writing a self-help book, but the original book has already been written; the Bible; it has the answers to everything that we live and breathe; why not let it work for you. The Word says, "Study to shew thyself approved unto God, a workman that needeth not to be ashamed, rightly dividing the word of truth," (2 Tim 2:15). Stop talking about it and be about it.

Thank God also for the five senses: Touch, Sight, Taste, Smell and Hearing, now use all of them as you communicate with your spouse to help you appreciate them more. Each plays an important part in our lives, but I think the touch of another is the most sensual part of a person, I think. God is so AMAZING!!! I can just remember that the touch of my spouse's hand would send shock waves all through my body, ultimately taking me to another planet. I recall it being soft, but firm enough to let me know he cared and appreciated me just by his touch all at the same time. The touch of the hand has the ability to heal or destroy, so use it wisely and correctly when corresponding with your mate. Never use it abusively, causing harm to them. What woman or man doesn't want to be touched by the person that they love or care for? WHOO HOO!!!! Even Jesus can attest to that, as just one touch from the hem of his garment made the woman whole. "And Jesus said, Who touched me? When all denied, Peter and they that were with him said, Master, the multitude throng thee and press thee, and sayest thou, Who touched me? And Jesus said, Somebody hath touched me: for I perceive that virtue is gone out of me," (Luke 8:45-46). He knew that he had been touched and there was something different that he had felt at that very moment; that someone had been healed as a result of it. Simply amazing, simply amazing.

Next there is sight, the ability to fix your eyes on an object; in this case the object is your special person. When you see him/her coming through the door, down the street, etc it should put a smile on your face that lights up the world or a room in no time flat; just the glimpse of them should leave a lasting thought in your mind throughout the day or night, or until you see them again. It should be so illuminating that even if you were blind, your brain would still send a signal giving you an image of what they look like vividly, and respond to what you remembered. "I want to see that person coming through the door every time." Ok, Saints, give me a few minutes to collect my thoughts, as I was having a brief moment, just thinking about my special person.

With taste being the third of the five; you should be so in tuned to your spouse or special person that you could also image what they would taste like if they were your favorite fruit or dish.; do they leave a sweet, salty, sour, or bitter taste in your mouth because of their attitude or do they remind you of the sweetest fruit drink from an exotic island in paradise. I'm sure you all have made that comment about "something looking so good that you could taste it." Well, that's exactly what I'm talking about. The taste of your person should also be significant to you. It's like the sense by which the flavor or savor of things is perceived when they are brought into contact with the tongue; implying a pleasing scent as well as taste or flavor, and connotes enjoyment in tasting. "O taste and see that the LORD is good: blessed is the man that trusteth in him." - Psalm 34:8

Smell and taste kind of goes hand-in-hand; taste is not the flavor; however, flavor does include the smell of a food as well as its taste. The definition of smell is to perceive something by its odor or scent. When you spend time with a person you begin to take on their scent, you know when their in the room, again sending a shock wave to your brain that reminds you of them. A sweet aroma, that sends a sensual feeling all though your body as well. Just the mere scent of their fragrance turns you on, even when their not in the room. As if to say, "she or he left a lasting scent" or ''I can't seem to forget you. Your Windsong stays on my mind." The slogan used to describe Prince Matchabelli's Windsong perfume from 1987, now, that's a blast from the past. The breeze of their scent just drives you CraZy, immediately bringing them into where you are even in their absence.

Finally, Hearing; just to hear their voice is like "a perfect verse over a tight beat, as quoted from another favorite movie of mine; "Brown Sugar - 1998." And can also remind one of romantic music or a soft whisper to your ear. Webster describes it as the faculty or sense by which sound is perceived. Hearing is all about vibration. Proverbs 15:1, says "A soft answer turneth away wrath; But a grievous word stirreth up anger."

That's how we should speak to our spouses or love ones, softly, not harsh, loud or abrupt. We should speak peace and love letting them know that we sincerely care about them and their wellbeing. It's all in how we say it that will keep them there or turn them away. Just the sound of your person's voice on the phone can calm your spirit; it could also change a major decision. Speak life and not death into your situation, your life and to your spouse or special person.

In the process of developing that long-lasting relationship, I had a woman of wisdom by the name of Jenny Boren, who has over 35 years of married life experience to share something with me that might help you as well; and it goes a little something like this. She said to just PRAY and gave me the following breakdown of PRAY from a session she taught:

Pray	Respect	Attitude	Yourselves
Pray without ceasing. I Thessalonians 5:17	Nevertheless do ye also severally love each one his own wife even as himself; and let the wife see that she fear her husband. Ephesians 5:33	Put on therefore, as God's elect, holy and beloved, a heart of compassion, kindness, lowliness, meekness, longsuffering. Colossians 3:12	Wherefore if any man is in Christ, he is a new creature: the old things are passed away; behold, they are become new. II Corinthians 5:17
Pray and ask God to bless your marriage. Pray he will draw you and your husband closer. Pray you will be desirable to your husband. Pray for your husband, and finally, Thank and Praise God for your husband.	It should be mutual. Don't put him down; instead be best friends to one another. Regard; favor; esteem; heed; gaze upon.	Look at yourself, are you being open minded. Always go to him in a calm manner. Try to listen and understand his point of view. Never give up on him, if he doesn't respond, keep trying.	Take time to be alone. Talk about things other than the kids. Talk about your relationship. Listen to him and share what's important to you with him.

These are simple, and it's funny how we miss the boat every time because we simply don't practice the basic things. She went on to share what women like, from their spouses as well, so you brothers better take note:

Women like it when their husbands:
- Hold their hands or hug them
- Affection without sex
- When you share your feelings
- Tell them about your day
- Listen to them
- Repeat back what they say, so they know you are listening
- Say to her you could never do her job
- Admit when you're wrong and ask for forgiveness
- Be the spiritual leader
- Praise them in public as well as in private
- Value their opinions

In closing, if your relationship and person are important to you then I encourage you to do all you can to work through your issues and build a long-lasting and loving relationship with that person. Know that a true relationship cannot exist unless you truly give of yourself. Remember that love is divine and it never dies.....and when you feel yourself drifting or confused remember these words "Love suffereth long, and is kind; love envieth not; love vaunteth not itself, is not puffed up, doth not behave itself unseemly, seeketh not its own, is not provoked, taketh not account of evil; rejoiceth not in unrighteousness, but rejoiceth with the truth; beareth all things, believeth all things, hopeth all things, endureth all things. Love never faileth: but whether there be prophecies, they shall be done away; whether there be tongues, they shall cease; whether there be knowledge, it shall be done away." - I Corinthians 13:4-8. Love is a gift and will always be something that you show or give to another. It is a lasting and memorable act. Someone asked just the other day if a relationship could last for a lifetime, I advised that it was possible; but you must honor and respect one another with your thoughts, words, and actions. As well as including the following ingredients from both partners to keep it intact:

RECIPE FOR A LONG-LASTING RELATIONSHIP

From the Kitchen of Jeanette Espinoza

Ingredients: Initial attraction, genuine interest, increasing desire, infatuation, yearning, respect, trust, understanding, patience, sense of humor, fun getaways, honesty, loyalty, and love.

Grab the biggest bowl in your cabinet and measure out 2 tablespoons of initial attraction and genuine interest. Slowly mix in 2/3 cups of increasing desire and infatuation, and pour yearning generously on top of your mixture.

Add 1 heaping cup of respect, 2 cups of trust and understanding, and 3 cups of patience. Add a cup and 1/2 of sense of humor and fun getaways.

Mix in 5 cups of honesty and loyalty and blend LOVE throughout all the ingredients.

Bake at a cool, calm, and collected temperature so that you can smell the patience simmering in your dish and serve generous helpings to your loved one with a warm smile and a gentle hugs on the side.

Add kisses to taste :) It would also be good to have these lying around to help keep things in proper perspective as well: Hope, Communication and Compatibility.

"Little does become MUCH once it's placed
In the MASTER'S hands."

A Poem
"EVERYBODY, SOMEBODY, ANYBODY, AND NOBODY"
Anonymous

This is a little story about four people named

Everybody, Somebody, Anybody, and Nobody.

There was an important job to be done and

Everybody was sure that Somebody would do it.

Anybody could have done it, but Nobody did it.

Somebody got angry about that because it was Everybody's job.

Everybody thought that Anybody could do it, but Nobody realized that

Everybody wouldn't do it.

It ended up that Everybody blamed Somebody when

Nobody did what Anybody could have done.

చ్రిం

Hopefully you or your partner doesn't take on any of these characteristics,

because if you do, I assure you that nothing will get done.

About the Author

~ Sheila King Knight ~

A native of Houston, TX, Sheila King Knight is also an accomplished singer, local theatre actress, and now adds author and writer to her list of credits, with her newly released book: "Life's Little Lessons - GOOD, bad, or InDiFfErEnT That Get You from Here to There." She operates a Christian Non-profit Platform called DYRArts which works with inner-city kids offering them an opportunity to get involved with the arts in their community by providing workshops, seminars and showcases from a Christian perspective. She's a member of Purpose Word Church in Lawrenceville, GA., where she's involved in Worship & Arts Ministries. She also serves as Assistant Chief Servant to the Renaissance Church in Lithonia, GA., an alternative to worshipping on Sundays, where they deliver **"A Real Message for A Real People in A Real World - Building a Youth Empire"** in their "Saturday Night Live" Services. She is answering the Clarion call on her life to sing God's Praises in season and out of season, as well as living her best life possible through test, trial and tribulation, but being totally honest and accountable to God, herself and others for her actions in relationships as a whole; Debut CD coming soon.

Email: sdyrocks2@yahoo.com

SHEILA & FRIENDS TERMINOLOGY

Over the years, my friends and I have been a part of theater, and other fun groups that have opened up our creative and artistic thinking allowing us to come up with some terms or a way of speaking to one another that keeps us laughing until we cry. We would like to
introduce some of those terms to you...Hope you enjoy.

Ah Lie or Ah Lee Lee - self explanatory

Agnes/Joseph - when someone is not listening for understanding and you keep having to explain to them over and over which makes you aggravated...instead of calling them by their name, you call them "Agnes"...cause they seem like a different person to you at the moment.

At Pause or Grieved - disbelief in something that has happened or surprised by a situation or issue; as in taken aback by it - "you would place your hand over your heart and say, why, I'm at Pause or Grieved."

Awwwww - using this term before a word enhances the expression of the word you just used, as it was important and meant something or you wouldn't have said it....Awwwww expression!!!

Cancel All Resees - means to cancel all reservation. If someone comes to you and ask you to do something promising and you're not in agreement, you can say "cancel all resee".....cause it ain't gone happen. You reserved the wrong trip. Awwwww wrong!

Dashing Through The Snow - speeding, in a hurry to get somewhere because you're late.

Dat Oughta Holja - after making a smart remark to a person, you immediately say, "Now, dat oughta holja."

Dosie Doe - when you are driving along side another car in the next lane prohibiting another vehicle to pass.

Dumb Dora - we call this a person who's having a blonde moment without the luxury of having had blonde hair. Just a dumb bunny, or dummy as in "Dumb Dora the Explorer"....I don't believe he/she just did that or said that." The deer in the headlight look or it just leaves your mouth standing wide open because you can't find the words to say to explain what just happened.

Goot-tevening - another way of saying have a good evening.

Hooped - laughing real hard at a situation.

If you had handled that - when a decision or something comes back on you that you should have handled or taken care of, that leaves you shamed or embarrassed, then this statement is made. As in to say, "If you had handled that they wouldn't be calling back now."

I've been put out of better places...... - this term is used when someone has asked you to leave. For example" you don't have to go home, but you do have to leave this place", then you would say, " Well, I've been put out of better places… And they can reply, but this is a first for this place."

Looking wise and other-wise - having a dazed, confused or lost look on your face; as if to say, "I saw Sheila the other day looking wise and other-wise."

Moved on or closure - when you're arguing or in disagreement with someone and you've made your statement and are finished, but the other person wants to continue, but you don't....you simply say, "I've moved on." Or you can say, "I have closure" and turn and walk away."

News of someone passing - when you get the news that someone has passed, you immediately make the statement that "people are dying who has never died b4; of course they have never died before, because it just happened."

Pausing for a moment of silence - in remembrance of someone who's passed on or a special time, that no longer exist. You'd pause for a moment of silence in memory of the person or place.

Poopalicious - use it during a sensitive or embarrassing moment, as in to say, "Awwwww poo poo or poopalicious, I'm so sorry to hear that." A term of endearment; derived from Poo Poo.

Sweet - This is the opposite of the characteristic of sugar, honey, or nice. It actually means not good to us, as in to say "that dress that she has on is sweeeeeeeeeeeeeet, she had no business wearing, and it's not attractive on her."

Side Eye - >: - meaning I'm giving you that look from out of the corner of my eyes.

The Last - meaning, you were wrong for saying or doing whatever you just did.

Too Many Things - you're trying to hard or you're doing too much all at the same time, and not getting anything accomplished.

Too The Flo' - someone giving you that look and with their eyes; they take you all the way down to the floor, as in to say, "No she didn't just take me to the floor with her eyes."

What's that you breatheth? - When you catch someone giving you that look, but they won't verbally said anything to you, you give them that same look back and ask; "what's that you breatheth?" as to say, "You got something you wanna say?"

Whoa - when someone is slained in the spirit. Nuff Sed!!!

Wally Werl - another way of saying Wal-Mart.

⚜

*Life is a journey, so much transpires, you have to
"just write it down." Don't forget to review it from
time-to- time to see how you've grown.*

Journal

———✦———

"Life's Little Lessons - GOOD, bad, or InDiFfErEnT
That Get You from Here to There"

"Life's Little Lessons - GOOD, bad, or InDiFfErEnT That Get You from Here to There"

"Life's Little Lessons - GOOD, bad, or InDiFfErEnT
That Get You from Here to There"

ENDNOTES

All Scripture quotations are taken from Holy Bible, American Standard Version, (ASV) Copyright © 1901.

Unless otherwise indicated, definitions are taken from Dictionary.com.

- http://family-law.lawyers.com/divorce/grounds-for-divorce-irreconcilable-differences.html

- Chester D. T. Baldwin

- http://www.lyricsmode.com/lyrics/r/rude_boys/undefined/lyrics/r/rude_boys/written_all_over_your_face.html

- Shaking my head, http://pc.net/slang/meaning/smh

- http://www.steveharveytv.com/s2-steves-relationship-advice/

- http://www.weddedyourway.com/traditional-i-do-vows.html

- https://www.biblegateway.com/passage/?search=Matthew+7%3A12&version=ESV

- Hamlet Act 1, scene 3, 78-82, http://www.enotes.com/shakespeare-quotes/thine-own-self-true

- Rollin on the floor laughing out loud, http://www.urbandictionary.com/define.php?term=rotflol

- http://alt-usage-english.org/excerpts/fxenquir.html

- http://www.oxforddictionaries.com/definition/english/you-can't-have-your-cake-and-eat-it-too

"Life's Little Lessons - GOOD, bad, or InDiFfErEnT
That Get You from Here to There"

- Acts 13:22

- 2 Cor 12:7

- http://www.azlyrics.com/lyrics/maryjblige/reallove.html

- http://apps.leg.wa.gov/rcw/default.aspx?cite=5.28&full=true

- The final difficulty in a series; the last little burden or problem that causes everything to collapse. http://idioms.thefreedictionary.com/the+straw+that+broke+the+camel's+back

- Proverbs 6:27

- Slang for a bad situation or problem. http://www.urbandictionary.com/define.php?term=sitchiation

- http://www.imdb.com/title/tt0042192/

- http://www.azlyrics.com/lyrics/arethafranklin/respect.html

- http://www.happychild.org.uk/nvs/cont/stories/aesopsfables/page0017.htm

- The illusion of having previously experienced something actually being encountered for the first time.

- http://www.americanrhetoric.com/MovieSpeeches/moviespeechmacolmxharlem.html

- http://www.imdb.com/title/tt0109830/trivia?tab=qt&ref_=tt_trv_qu

- Intense, burning desire. http://onlineslangdictionary.com/meaning-definition-of/jones

- A seductive woman who lures men into dangerous or compromising situations.

- http://www.merriam-webster.com/dictionary/femme%20fatale

- http://www.azlyrics.com/lyrics/icet/donthatetheplaya.html

- John 8:32

- http://www.goodreads.com/quotes/9821-i-did-then-what-i-knew-how-to-do-now

- http://www.azlyrics.com/lyrics/slythefamilystone/thesamethingmakesyoulaughmakesyoucry.html

- http://www.azlyrics.com/lyrics/brianmcknight/backatone.html

- Hebrews 12:1

- http://www.azlyrics.com/lyrics/beyonceknowles/crazyinlove.html

- http://www.azlyrics.com/lyrics/bettywright/nopainnogain.html

- Matthew 28:20, Hebrews 13:5

- Matthew 22:37

www.ingramcontent.com/pod-product-compliance
Lightning Source LLC
Chambersburg PA
CBHW060252100426
42742CB00011B/1729